Messeria, And O... ...ins...

Eliza Down

Nabu Public Domain Reprints:

You are holding a reproduction of an original work published before 1923 that is in the public domain in the United States of America, and possibly other countries. You may freely copy and distribute this work as no entity (individual or corporate) has a copyright on the body of the work. This book may contain prior copyright references, and library stamps (as most of these works were scanned from library copies). These have been scanned and retained as part of the historical artifact.

This book may have occasional imperfections such as missing or blurred pages, poor pictures, errant marks, etc. that were either part of the original artifact, or were introduced by the scanning process. We believe this work is culturally important, and despite the imperfections, have elected to bring it back into print as part of our continuing commitment to the preservation of printed works worldwide. We appreciate your understanding of the imperfections in the preservation process, and hope you enjoy this valuable book.

MESSERIA,

AND OTHER POEMS.

By ELIZA DOWN.

LONDON:
JARROLD & SONS, 3, PATERNOSTER BUILDINGS.

ERRATA.

Page 9, line 2—*For* "An" *read* "The"—thus,
    The aged monarch's cry, "My son!

Page 42, line 18—*For* "shade" *read* "slade"—thus,
    Girdled a beauteous grassy slade,

Page 134, line 7—*For* "Through which" *read* "Which through"—thus,

Which through the sorrow-clouds of madness shines

CONTENTS.

	Page
MESSERIA	5
TO A BUTTERFLY	82
THE NAIAD	84
MAY	87
THE CUP OF TEARS	88
TO THE VIOLET	90
THE ECHO	91
AN EVENING VISION	93
THE GIRL AT THE FOUNTAIN	96
TO A CUCKOO	98
THE CHILD CHRIST	99
THE HARVEST MOON	101
ROSA MAY	102
THE PRIMROSE	103
THE PIXIE DANCE	105
THE LILY OF THE VALE	108
THE BIRDS	111

Contents.

	Page
To a Child	113
To the Primrose	115
The Naiad	117
Alice	118
To the Snowdrop	119
The Fairy	121
Titania	123
Timon's Grave	125
Fidele	127
Ariel	130
Ophelia	132
Miranda	135
The Well of Samaria	138
List of Subscribers	161

Messerin.

Part I.

THE monarch saw with glance of pride
  His king-like son sit on his steed,
  Which pawed the ground with haughty hoof
As in disdain. He saw with joy
His beautiful belovèd ride,
The foremost of the courtly train,
The noblest of the knightly band!
The courser's glittering trappings swept
The ground, and soft the silver bells
Upon its arched and glossy neck
Made music with each step: he rode
Apart, advanced before the rest,
And led the courtly cavalcade
Beside the sounding main. His face
Was beautiful with youthful grace,
And on his brow a regal power

Did sit, and mark him as a lord
Of men.   Upon his shoulders flowed
Rich locks of paly gold, while beamed
From those deep eyes of azure hue
A proud yet tender soul! his crest
Was plumed with feathers gay, which waved
And flamed with every passing breeze;
And shone the jewelled robe he wore
Resplendent in the noontide light!
Downward toward the beach they swept,
Where, sounding, broke upon the shore
The long blue wave; and loud afar,
Deep ocean in its mighty bed
Heaved up a multitudinous voice.
Gaily the courtly party rode,
Sweet laughter rang upon the ear,
And to the lips the light jest leapt
From happy hearts at rest.   The sea
With heaving bosom lay, and rolled
Its billows forth, which on them wore
The crested foam, like beards of snow.

It was the noon of summer's day;
The wind with kisses warm did creep
Among the embowering shades, and all
The fanning leaves with murmurs soft,
His steps adored: from out the woods

That lined the margin of the shore,
He came, and bore upon his wings
The stolen sweets of many a flower!
Noon in its golden ecstacy
Lay dreaming in the ambient air,
When in the silence rang a voice
Aërial, mystical, and sweet,
A solitary voice in song;
It rose from out the nearer wave,
And floated on the stilly air,
A strain as sweet as sings the bird
Of night, when she in shadowy grove
Doth sit, and pour her amorous soul.
Low, soft, and sweet at first it rose,
Then louder as it upward swelled
That strain of syren witchery!
So sings the wild white swan, when she
With awful jubilant voice doth chant
Her own death-dirge, floating away
In solemn music to her doom!

Why spurs the Prince his haughty steed?
Why bounds he forward to the main?
The wavelets lave his courser's feet,
The ocean-foam is on his face!
Far out at sea a syren sits,
The low-bowed waves in worship kiss

Her white and dainty form; she sings
And shakes her amber locks and lures
To her the enamoured youth! her hair
Is wreathed with bright sea-flowers, and
 strings
Of pearl about her breast are twined,
A lovely Peri of the deep
She glows, and dazzles with her charms!
She half-way from the sea upreared
Her gleaming form, then slowly dipped
Below the wave, and passed from sight!
But from beneath ascended still
The wild melodious song, and o'er
The waters rang   The haughty steed,
As at the sound of battle blast,
Rears his proud neck and forward bounds;
He snorts for joy, his eyeballs flash;
With mighty limbs the current's strength
He stems, and bears his rider through
The rushing waves! Far out at sea,
Where from the bosom of the deep
Ascends the wild melodious chant,
A white and jewelled hand is raised,
A female hand, its fingers clasped
With golden rings. The panting horse
Toils 'gainst the rush of billows wild,
Straining toward the beckoning hand.

Then rang a cry of anguish loud,
An aged monarch's cry, "My son!
My son! mine only son, forbear!"
The rider and the foaming steed
Strike through the seething billows wild,
The thundering waves about them roll—
The mighty waves above them close.

The rider and the curbless horse
Went down: the sea her bosom cleft,
And opening, showed through her abyss
A pathway wide, with glittering walls
Of chrysolite on either side
Enclosed, a pathway broad and smooth,
Where the triumphant chariot wheels
Of great sea-gods in pomp might roll,
When all the nymphs of Neptune's train
Their proud procession swell. With flowers
Of varied hue the way was strewn,
And all the pavement seemed to glow
As if with precious stones inlaid:
Sapphire and pearl and amethyst,
The emerald and topaz pale,
Mosaic work inwrought, and all
The odorous ruby of the rose
Infused its tints therein, and made
Adornment rich. 'Long the proud way

A solitary isle which rose
Like a cybelè from the sea.
Limpid and calm the waters lay
At foot of the ascent on which
They stood,—a far extending flood.
The waves with gentle murmurs flowed
Tender and low, like infants' breath.
High over all, the ocean-heaven
Unrolled its splendours pale, the moon
Glided on high—the queenly moon,
With vestal stars about her car—
And downward cast her reflex pure,
Turning to silver at her touch
The far expanse of waters vast!
Wooded the isle, of circular shape,
And towering upward to a mount
Which on its brow did seem to wear
A dim tiara of great towers,
High pinnacles which cast a light
From off their spires upon the space
Below, till the whole isle appeared
To lie upon the waves, a pale
Gigantic orb of lustrous light!
The merman leader gave the word
Of high command, and instant wheeled
The glittering host; in serried ranks,
On either side the Prince they rode,

And all the mighty throated pipes
Of war gave forth their lofty notes.
Downward they passed, nor paused, until
They came where ocean's tramway verged
Upon the nether flood: then spoke
The great sea lords, "Across the waves
We pass, but fear not thou, oh Prince!
On her sustaining breast the sea
Shall bear thy courser and thyself
Secure: firm as the adamant
She turns at word of ours."

                       They passed
The beachèd margin of the flood:
Their giant steeds with wings upraised,
Which caught the whirlwind in their stroke,
Boldly put forth, and undismayed,
The Prince's charger moved, 'mong these
His brethren of the sea. He caught
Their fiery ardour, and sprung forth
Among the foremost rank; in pomp
Of glittering panoply arrayed,
They rode, the horsemen of the deep:
They, on their shoulders flung their shields
Of bossy gold, great globes of light,
Which burned, and cast a fiery track
Along the paler wave: it was

As if the heaven had shook her host
Of stars upon the deep! and as
The forest trees that shower their leaves
Upon the paths, so numberless
That mighty band! so passed they on
With swiftest speed to the bright isle,
Their journey's bourn, of their great Queen
The chosen residence, for there
Old ocean, in his own domain,
Did form for her a garden large
And fair, seat of delicious bliss,
A flowery Paradise! soft gales
With zephyrus' wings bore from the shore
The spicy aroma; rich scents,
That in their native groves distilled,
Drowned the lulled senses with delights—
Intoxicating sweets; and sounds
Of music rippled o'er the wave,
Harpings with chant of syren voice
Accompanied. The adoring deep
That bore the orb of glory on
Her breast, kissed with her tender waves
The golden sands, and thence fell back
With murmurs pleased to her confines.
Gained the fair isle, their wished-for port,
The foremost horsemen leapt from off
Their wingèd steeds, and strode the strand

With steps of pride; with shouts that woke
The reverbering caves, they gave command
To their battalions bright, to form
In circle round the sacred isle,
Abiding under guard. They heard
And straight obeyed; band after band
Defiled, and swiftly belted round
The holy mount; as in the heavens
The moon does sometimes show, with pale
And vaporous rings surrounded, so
Orb beyond orb, the sons of light
Outspread them on the azure deep,
Around that moon-like sphere.

                              "Behold,"
The knights of ocean said, "behold
Our favoured isle: here sits our Queen,
Our lady in immortal prime,
And many a fair and fragrant clime
Her sceptred rule obeys! her fame
Folds in the swelling deep; her name
The mighty Neptune on his lips
Bears to the bounds where his confines
Do border earth's. Welcome, oh Prince,
To this fair place! to thee we give
Our loves in measure large and free;
Our home and fortunes share!"

					Then spake
The Prince. "Oh, sons of ocean, great
Your natures, and your loves as great;
With you I measure courtesy,
With you in my delights will vie;
Mine eye with the rich scene is charmed,
The sweet air gently fans my lips,
And wild delicious joy bounds through
My veins with the soft rapturous touch.
Ne'er saw I vision beautiful
As this fair isle, with radiant pomp
Begirt; the groves resonant with
The voice of song, flush with the buds
Of leafy spring, and all the vales
With verdure smile: if the deep sea
Attractions such as these can boast,
Here in faërie will I rest,
And the proud home from whence I came,
The palace of mine ancestors,
Forget. Lead on, oh mightiest peers!
I follow in your steps."

					The isle
With amphitheatre of hills,
Wooded with trees of stateliest growth,
Extended far: dim colonnades
Outstretched, in lines, tier above tier,

To where the lofty mount sat crowned
With its great central gem of light,
The palace of the ocean queen,
With glittering cupolas which shed
A lustrous glory round ; in bowers
More green, satyr or fawn ne'er played,
Nor dryad sported in the shade
With hairy Pan! umbrageous woods
With flowery meads between, made there
A scene of sylvan loveliness,
A soft arcadia of delight.
Lo! where the crisp'd and golden sand
Melted into the emerald turf,
An altar stood—an altar hewn
As of the solid rock, of huge
Colossal size. No sacrifice
Did smoke thereon, but on it piled
Were flowers, such as the deep sea bears,
The fruitage of her inmost womb,
And newly drawn, dripping and wet
An ocean offering.

    From thence
A winding path by slow ascent
Led up among the embowering groves,
With ferny growth on either side
Fringed and adorned : up the smooth path

The mermen lords then led the way.
The Prince his charger rode; but they
On foot equalled his swiftest speed,
And kept with graceful ease his side
With powers untasked.

     Not as on earth,
Where the pale moonbeams touch all things
With paleness like themselves, but here
With fulgent beam the queen of night
Brought out distinct the varied hues,
But softer and more spiritually pure.
Dreamlike and tender was the scene,
Ethereal loveliness, in form
Such as might haunt a poet's sleep,
But never dawned on mortal sight!
The flowery growth of many a land
In beauty bloomed; trees of the east
With Europe's forest grandeurs mixed
In the umbrageous woods; the flower
And fruitage of the tropics here.
With gorgeous tints luxuriant glowed
The flora of the north, with all
Her pale and virgin hues; the palm
With plumy crest of pride uprose;
The aloe and the prickly cactus,
The trees of Araby, which drop

With fragrant gums, exhalèd sweets.
The banan, with her branches cleft
The yielding ground, and made herself
A family; and by her stood
The stately oak with shadowing boughs,
Hoary with his antiquity!
Springtide it seemed, for the meek buds
Of early spring softly put forth,
The pale and delicate primrose peered
From out her tuft of deep green leaves,
Timid and young: yet golden ripe
The gorgeous fruits of autumn glowed,
The trailing vine her clusters hung
Low on the ground—purple and flushed:
Nor solitary swelled the vine,
Conceptive ere her time, but groves
Of orange and of citron bore
Their treasures, large and fully ripe;
The nectarous pine, and downy peach
There amplest fruitage wore: the fig
And olive riped, and freely gave
The loaded branches to the hand.
Now gained the higher mount, a scene
Of grandeur opened on the view:
Girt with its vernal glories round,
The ocean palace towered on high
With pinnacles which pricked the air

And throbbed with beams of light: so shines
The hoary summit of Mont Blanc,
When on his snow-wrapped brow he wears
The brightness of the ascended sun.
Mighty its size, its portals vast,
And front a blaze of flashing jewels.
On either side its massive gates
A wingèd lion stood, and kept
Unceasing guard; far round it spread
A fair expanse of velvet sward,
An emerald lawn with flowers bedecked,
Spontaneous birth of the pure earth,
Each hour in loveliness renewed.
The banks with new-shed roses blushed,
Dropped from a thousand boughs, which wore
Their crimson glories thickly still.
Central in the fair plain there rose
A fountain clear and bright, which cast
Its crystal jets aloft in clouds
Of silvery spray, thence falling back
Diffused in many a sinuous rill
O'er all the verdurous mead, and gave
Its freshness to the receptive earth.
And lo! around it lightly danced
An hundred naked sea-nymphs, white
As lily of the May! they moved
In mystic dance, not without song,

Graceful and wild, with leaf-crowned brows,
Fair daughters of the sea, that seemed
More lovely than the maids of earth!

The mermen peers their bugles raised,
And blew a long resounding blast
In signal of return.   Full soon
From out the green and leafy bowers
Came many a troop of forest nymphs.
In graceful dance, with song they moved,
With airy and harmonious steps.
Loose garlands in their hands they brought;
With these they crowned their ocean lords,
While chants of victory they raised:
But first and chief, the son of earth
They hailed, and low before him bowed
The knee; creatures more fair ne'er knelt
In reverence at mortal's foot
In sign of lowly adoration.
He from his charger leapt, and gave
To the fair Peris at his side
Becoming courtesy.   Then spoke
The loveliest of the ocean maids,
A nereid young, with flowing hair,
Which swept her breast to where the zone
Her white and stainless robe confined.
"Hail to thee, Prince! to thee we bring

The salutations of our Queen;
The chosen of our lady thou,
She in her palace waits thy long
Desired approach!" Then passed she on
And led the way with flowerets showered
Before his steps. O'er blushing beds
Of roses dropped he walked, with song
And dance encompassed round; they wound
In proud procession o'er the plain,
To the broad palace steps: the gates
Of orient pearl swung open wide,
Resounding music sweet, while gave
The guarding lions on each side
Free way. Within those lofty halls
Of ocean pride they came, where, girt
With all her mightiest potentates,
The sovereign of the seas sat throned.
The great sea-gods, whose hoary locks
Flowed o'er their mantles green, were there,
The hierarchies of the deep.
With them in ranks the minor powers
Stood ranged, in proud and courtly pomp,
Long trains of Oceänus' sons
Assembled there, with nereids mixed,
Lovely and fair. Lofty and high
The palace walls, and studded thick
With crystal gems, while silver lamps

From the bright ceiling hung, shed round
A tempered light, and fragrant burned,
With sweetest oils fed and supplied,
Filling with ceaseless aroma
Those grand and stately ocean halls.
Not Egypt, nor Assyria,
Not India, when she pours her wealth
Profuse, in showers of pearl and gold,
Magnificence so great could boast.
The tribute treasures of the earth
Might ne'er build up splendours so vast.
On throne of gold the sovereign sat,
Beneath a canopy of state,
Of cloth of gold, heavy and rich,
With diamonds gemmed. Moulded her form
Like some fine statue of a queen,
Wrought by a Grecian master's hand.
Her countenance, superbly proud,
Breathed majesty, save that the eyes,
Unutterably sweet, did tone
The enormous grandeur of the brow,
With soft and tender female grace.
The raven hair, which waving flowed
Upon her shoulders pure, was dewed
With ocean-pearls, and round her wrists
Were bracelets twined of orient gems.
The purple vesture that she wore,

Was from her shoulders thrown, and left
Her bosom bare down to the waist,
From whence it hung with lustres dight,
And lay in many a heavy fold
Upon the golden throne. Full orbed
Her breasts, and lovely as the teats,
At which a human mother feeds
Her loveliest babe; and seemed they such
As female breast that drips with milk
Upon the infant's lips. No crown
She wore, but from her regal brow
Great rays of light shot forth, and wreathed
A living diadem.

    The voice
Of song resounded through the halls;
The dulcimer, the pipe, and flute,
"All organs of sweet stop," gave forth
Their richest symphonies, sweet notes
Of joy.

   Before the lofty throne
Two shapes of glowing light there stood:
Great forms that towered—female and male—
Noble and god-like was the one,
Plumed like the herald Mercury;
And beautiful in port as he,

When lighted on Olympus' top,
He shakes the downy gold from off
His wingèd heels. The other wore
Upon her lips the sweets of spring,
And in her face such splendour glowed,
As flora wears in summer's prime.
With soft attractive grace she pleased;
Female her charms—a woman fair:
Lovely as naked Venus, when
She lay on beds of flowers supine,
Or when she, in mount Ida, strove
And won the beauty palm. So glowed,
So shone that lovely female thing.
She shook her glistering glory-robe,
And all her beauties bared. Anon
With stormful grandeur charged her brow,
And darted darkness from her eyes;
Then seemed she as the spirit of wrath,
Incarnate! He, on the other side,
Did vary oft his form sublime,
Leading her changes with his change:
And evermore he seemed to bend him
Forward, and on her breast to breathe,
Which rose, and heaved, and fell beneath
His breath, with its white hills of snow
With azure tinct.

     Of wind and wave
The twain great rulers, they, with powers
Mutual, enlinked.

     So throned, so girt
With all her mightiest potentates,
The majesty of ocean showed:
And raptures woke in him who knelt
Before her throne, a stranger there.
She bent her from her seat, and spoke
With voice mellifluous and soft,
"More glad than those that hail the morn
 In thine own vales of earth," she said,
"I greet thee here, oh, best beloved.
 Lo! the huge titans round my throne,
These shall thy fellows be; and all
The lovely maidens of my train
 Shall minister to thy delights;
Soft pleasures from their lips, more sweet
Than droppings of the honey comb,
For ever flow. In dance and song
The rosy hours shall glide; a dream
Of bliss in fairy land. Here rest,
And be the measure of thy joys
For ever heaped and full."

       He heard,
And was content; he sat him down
Low at the footstool of her feet.

PART II.

Around that verdurous seat of bliss
The softest airs of ocean breathed;
A region of perpetual peace,
Where storms came not. The gorgeous flowers
Blazed and illumined all the bowers
With hues more vivid than the scarf
That Iris wears, of rainbow dyes.
Beneath the bright moon's gliding beam
Most beautiful the scene had been,
For bud and leafy branch to her
Their greenness showed; and the young flower
Which closed awhile at evening's hour,
Opened with joy its dewy eye
With bosom bared, exhaling scents,
More glorious now when day arose,
And with its lambent splendours filled
Those soft and undulating vales.

The sun, now waxing to the noon,
His vapoury violet mantle flung
Over the dense umbrageous woods;
There on the banks of embrowned shade
The creeping vine with branches laid,
Grew big with fruit, and asphodels,
Hyacinths pale, and violets dim,
Spangled a soft luxurious couch,
Where Love in dreams of bliss might lie
In his immortal Psyche's lap.
Hither the bands of lovely nymphs
Who with the mermaid queen abode,
With soft enticements led the Prince;
And 'neath the green and swaying boughs,
While now the mounted sun rode high,
On thymy bed they made him rest;
While sweeter than the warbling flow
Of crystal fountains near at hand,
They trilled the soft ecstatic lay.
The silence of the noon was pleased,
And the sweet air did seem to hang
Upon the blissful strain enrapt,
More low, more sweet, more tender strains
Ne'er flowed from breast of philomel
In magic groves of Attica.
Tenebrous boughs of antique trees
From whence the pendant mosses hung,

A leafy canopy did weave
O'erhead; and underneath the low
And trailing vine her juicy breasts
Gave to the touch, swelling and ripe,
Nectars from her ambrosial veins
Distilled, to cool the feverish thirst
By the hot noon produced: so slid
The honeyed hours in dalliance sweet
In the unruffled summer calm,
Until the glowing orb of day
Dipped his red brow with vapours swathed,
Low in the western wave. Now came
The evening pale and grey; the mild
And dewy vesper star shone forth
With lucid beam: o'er all the hills
A silvery dimness seemed to come.
And cool and grateful swept the breeze
Over the emerald meads, while drops
Of moisture from the humid locks
Of eve shook off, softly distilled
Into the bosom of the flowers
Refreshment pure: they drank and slept,
Not as the flowers of earth, which close
Through the long night their lustrous eyes,
But in brief time, to gather strength
For double life, in one swift hour
Of balmy ocean rest, nor breath

Nor sound the holy stillness broke;
Deep silence lay upon the face
Of things, and bird and beast reposed.
In the clear sapphire depths now rose
The lustrous moon, and with her came
The stars; and at her bright uprising,
The island maids, gathered in troops,
With pœans hailed her beam. Now wore,
Touched by her silvery wand, the groves
Fresh splendours on their boughs, the meads
Laughed with expanded flowers, and all
The isle became enchanted ground,
Faëry scene of loveliness.
Within the woods in ferny glades
A million fire-flies flashed and danced,
Until the dim bowers shone and flamed
With those aërial gems of light!
The gorgeous bloom of tropic flowers
Showered o'er the mighty forest trees,
With magic tints more gorgeous glowed
'Neath the strange flash of living fire.
The orange and the lemon groves,
With bending boughs of clustered fruit,
With emeralds and rubies burned.
The moon with Venus at her side
Rode through the deepening azure skies,
And all the mustering host of stars

Gathered on high; the martial Mars
Shook the red rays from off his brow,
And sailed in pomp of fiery light.
Now, at the time of Dian's rise,
Her wonted hour, came forth the Queen
Of those fair realms; beside her moved
The mighty Tritons of the deep,
The hoary giants of olden time.
In chariot of gold she rode
With sapphires paved; milk white her steeds,
White as the snow; and from their manes
They shook the flaky brightness off.
The daughters of the sea-gods came,
Following her car, with chants of praise,
Triumphal song and dance: the wheels
Of her celestial chariot seemed
As set with blushing pearls, pale orbs,
In which the pink with whiteness vied;
And as they pressed the dewy mead,
The sounds of sweetest music rang
With every movement of their spheres.
At her right hand, the princely youth
Whom she from earth lately allured,
By syren strains her hand-maid sung,
She caused to sit, and on him shed
Benignant smiles—"Lo! see!" she said,
"How beautiful my ocean seat!

Come, taste the sweetness of the hour,
While tempered to the light of heaven,
The vales, the woods, the ocean smiles.
Mark you yon cataract's foaming fall
With rainbow wreathed, a glittering arch;
High on the craggy rock above
Stands the lone palm, in stately pride,
With golden-clustered fruitage crowned;
Tell me, canst thou conceive a sight
More grand, more beautiful than this!
Bound lightly o'er the ground, my steeds,
Roll swift, ye circling wheels of pearl,
And bear us to the sandy beach:
The curling waves break on the strand,
It is the time of evening tide."

So passed they onward to the shore;
And as the golden chariot rolled
Through those ambrosial groves, the nymphs
From all the forest glades came forth
With branching boughs of palms, and wreaths
Wove of the darker leaves of oak
Or pine, which in the way they strawed
In honour of their stately Queen.

The lustrous deep with rippling waves

Messeria.

Touched the smooth strand, while beetling
    cliffs,
Girdling with giant forms the beach,
Stood in relief against the sky,
Draped to the base with mantling moss,
Banks upon banks of glorious flowers.
The wild and white convolvulus
Hung there her pendant silver bells,
Commixed with many a gorgeous bloom,
And pale and feathery ferns.

                              Before
The rock-hewn altar near at hand
Were vestals clad in stoles of white;
The virgin daughters of the sea,
Who waited at the ocean shrine,
And heaped the verdurous sacrifice.
O'er the smooth strand the chariot rolled;
The proud steeds curbed, stayed in their
    course;
The nymphs and the illustrious peers
Gathered about their lady's car:
She rose, she stood erect, the wind
Waved back her dark and glossy hair,
Her deep eyes glowed, her bosom swelled,
Superb in majesty, in her
The mighty glory of the scene,

The grandeur of the sea and sky
Seemed welded into living form;
The deep gave forth its vassal-tribes
To offer homage to its Queen.
The dolphin in the wave that played
Made sport to please her eye; the bright
Star-fish leapt up with glittering scales,
Darting aloft in hoary light:
Leviathan, hugest of things,
Rolled his enormous bulk along,
And paid her court: the white sea-gull,
The wide-winged mighty albatross,
With birds of every wing that haunt
The bosom of the deep, or track
The ebbing wave in quest of prey,
Came circling round, and hung on high
Moveless and still, a diadem
Of outspread wings, a mighty crown
Of living things hung in the air
Aloft, in far expanding orb:
Nor more than wonted worship paid,
For oftentimes they thus adored
Their Queen, the lady of the sea.
The vestals from the altar came,
They glided o'er the glistening wave;
With choral symphonies they wound
Their way along the heaving main:

Then dived, and from the inmost womb
Of the deep sea, brought up the dank
And dripping weeds; as offerings meet,
These on the rock-hewn shrine they laid,
To the great ocean deity,
A sacrifice each morn and eve
Renewed. The sacred pile they heaped,
And sprinkling round the water-drops,
With voices raised in solemn chant,
The invisible spirit of the deep
Invoked. The moon, behind a bank
Of clouds, looked forth, paling her light;
The wind was hushed, the deep was mute,
The wave upon its curl hung poised,
Congealed and still. Then slowly rose
From out the watery abyss
A dusk and giant shape, a form
As of a god, wrapped in a robe
Of hoary clouds; erect he towered,
And came with vast and haughty strides
Toward the shore; his vapoury skirt,
With darkness fringed, trailed o'er the deep
With thunderous sound. So came he on:
His feet pressed on the glittering strand,
And the Sea-queen advanced to meet
Her lord, while bowed the host around.
"It is the spirit of the deep,"

They to the young prince said. "Behold!
It is the great Oceänus,
Whose presence as a mantle floats,
Covering the confines of the deep!"

"Hail, mighty sire!" the vestals sung;
"Primeval father, from whose loins
The tribes of ocean sprung, the great
And first begetter of all life.
Hail to thee, prime and chief of all
The Ocean-powers! And thou, no less
Majestic mother, at whose breast
Were nursed the first of things; whose teats
For ever full, do still sustain
Thy countless children of the deep!
She, whom the ancients meetly named
Goddess of love, and life, and beauty;
(Lo! love and life are one, for love
Is fountain of all being,) of thee
Came forth, when thy soft curling waves
Lipped the smooth earth with murmurous
    sound,
The rosy dawning saw her born,
What time the airy graces rose
With the sweet seasons linked in dance.
From thee, oh, great maternity,
Budded the earliest germs of life,

And still and undiminished breeds
Thy womb prolific its new growths."

As when the sun nearing his couch
In the dim purple occident
Parts the dense folds of heavy mist,
That veil his majesty, and shoots
His glory to the zenith's crown
In sudden beams, till the whole heaven
Is flushed and kindled far and wide;
So, from the robe of dusky clouds,
In which he shrouded up his essence,
Shone forth the god. The silent waves—
Silent erewhile in deepest awe—
Brake into voice; sublime he stood,
And from his awful front shot forth
Lightnings and splendours o'er the deep;
And o'er the fair reposing isle,
Sweet songs and music sounded from
The groves, and chanting voices ran
Along the deep, and rose from out
Her nethermost abyss.

      With pomp
Of solemn rites the island-host
Kept festival, and with the loud
Resounding trumps the echoes woke

Of the far hills, till all the woods
Gave forth in troops the sylvan nymphs
To worship at the sea-god's feet,
And aye around the altar wove
With songs the white-robed ministers,
The sacred mystic dance.
      So came
The majesty of the great deep,
Wrapped in his attributes of awe;
Thus oft from bands of darkness swathed
About his glory bared he the brow
Of deity:—thus came, and passed,
Even as he came in mystery.

 * * * * *

There, in the garden of the sea,
Where the perpetual summer glowed,
And on that bowery paradise
Shook down luxuriant tropic life,
The prince abode, nor knew one wish
Ungratified, for Nature there
Her soul in loveliness unveiled,
And eye and ear were satiate
With luscious scenes of sylvan beauty
And ever pleasant sounds; while day
And night ceased not the balmy gales

To shake their spoils abroad, and fill
The senses with their ecstasy
Of sweets.

PART III.

The night slid into morn;
The sun, from out the chaliced flowers,
Sipped the cold dews; the long white mists
Folding the heights dissolved, and day
Was ushered in.   Through the still glades,
When the first beams of morning broke,
Ocænia, with her chosen nymphs,
Oft roamed, or with her loud-voiced hounds
Rousing the echoes of the hills,
Chased she the fleet and antlered stag;
But, now the maidens of her train
Dismissed, she sought her favourite page,
The princely youth, her best beloved!
Within her halls he lay, nor yet
Awaked; his bared heroic breast,
Crossed with the brawny arms, where sloped
The muscle strong, spoke the proud knight,

In tilt and tournament unmatched,
The noblest son of chivalry
In Europe's courts!

                With breath more sweet
Than that of zephyr when he wakes
The violet sleeping in the shade,
She o'er him bent and kissed his brow.
"Awake, arise," she said, "the morn
Is up; let us among the flowers.
Come, seize the hour of dewy prime,
And wandering through the cultured groves,
Mark how the rich pomegranate blooms,
How swells the early tender bud,
How bends the loaded branch with fruit!"

He rose and followed in her steps;
She led the way o'er the smooth plain,
To the fair trellised bowers, where hung
Convolved the star-like flowers, great eyes
Of light! orchids all hues, pale white,
And crimson deep, like globes of blood.
The meeker flora on the ground
Crept forth with lowly buds, and leaves
Sombre or bright; unfed with rains,
The fertile earth brought forth her seed
Conceptive by the sun, and touched

By him her unpolluted breast
Yielded its dews, and of itself
Nourished the inward growth, she shook
Her treasures forth, boundless and free;
Splendours unmeasured poured at will.
The vine, with ripened clusters, wooed
The hand, nor less the date, or balls
Of gold the orange showed, or figs
That hung upon the loaded boughs:
They passed and plucked, nor scarcely plucked,
For on their hand Nature showered down
Her gifts unasked, dropping her fruits
Upon them as they passed.

                                The streams
Rippling, flowed through the sylvan shades
With a continuous murmuring,
Low, sweet like whisperings of love.
Through the arcadian groves, well pleased,
The knight followed his lady's steps;
Often they paused, and moved aside
The tasselled boughs crossing their path,
Which in their faces tossed a snow
Of blossoms white, and glittering showers
Of perfumed dew; within the bowers
They passed mid grey and antique trees;

Knee-deep in flowers they went, and as
The lustrous robeOcænia wore,
Over the odorous herbage trailed,
The air waxed faint with rich perfumes,
The heavy purple buds bent down
To touch her hand, and the pressed breast
Of earth its adoration gave
To her its Queen: smiling she stood,
Tempering her majesty with grace
Of gentleness; nor greater seemed,
As o'er her proud knight's low-bent head
Her fingers strayed, in fond caress,
Dappling his hair, than the young nymphs,
Her handmaids, who with him oft roamed,
And on his steps attendant hung.
They came within a cirque of trees,
Which, with their giant shadowy arms,
Girdled a beauteous grassy shade,
There paused, and on the emerald turf
They sat them down; not far remote
Was there a lovely caverned grot
Hid in an overhanging cliff,
Its entrance screened by drooping boughs.
Dusky and sacred was the place,
By spell preserved inviolate,
To Ocænia consecrate.
No foot e'er entered there, nor nymphs,

Nor the immortals trod that path;
But she alone went in, and with
The genius of the place communed.
There, when the moon her silver shaft
Relumed, the maids of ocean sang,
Or framed the glorious dance; aye-flowing
Waters issued from thence, and o'er
The mead in holy streams diverged,
The spangled mosses ever fresh
Preserved. O'er the soft delicate marge,
With ferns and flowers and ivy growth
Tangled and massed, the waters leapt,
Sprinkling their glistening drops around.
The nereids in that beauteous spot
Oft played, or braided in their hair
The flowers there plucked, such flowers as won
By potent spell, the love of him
The ocean-virgins sought, but none
Within the guarded cave might make
Resort; neither of those who, linked
In troops, wandered the isle, nor these
Elect, the daughters of the gods,
Who by their sovereign's chariot ran,
When she at eventide rode forth,
Gracing her proud triumphal way
With dance and song, her chosen nymphs

Of lovely loveliest they.   No sound
Discordant broke the stillness there—
No voice, or hoarse or sweet, save song
From lips of Oceäniedes
Poured out beneath the vestal moon
What time she rose, but from within
The sacred cave might he who bent
His ear low at the entrance hear
Sometime, a tender whisper rise,
And through the grotto softly run
A sound like airy echo's plaint,
Mourning her love, as mystic sweet
As melody in the sea-shell,
When inland far it lies.

      The Prince
Sat at his lady's feet; and she,
With hands clasped round his brow, gazed
 down
Into his eyes, while half reclined
He leaned upon her knee: awhile
They thus in silence sat, and spoke
No word: not yet the air had lost
Its coolness, nor the ground her dews;
But soft and fresh she on her face
Unshorn her virgin graces wore.
At length the knight the silence broke

With measured words tender and low:
"Lovely," he said, "the morn, so calm,
So beautiful, it breathes but peace,
But peace and deep extatic love.
All things are here of love, the flowers,
The trees, the mantled crags have caught
His glow, the air with his sweet breath
Is faint with rapture; rich and clear
His notes swell out in song of birds,
Warbling from thousand thickets round.
All things of him receive; mark you
Yon pale white bud upon the stalk,
A perfect bud,—a tintless rose!
See, while the sweet south wind doth blow
Its petals crimson with its breath,
And the white drops of dew thereon,
With the red glory underneath
Incarnadine; upon my heart
Like yonder splendour on the rose,
The sweetness of a dream yet lies,
(A dream from which thou call'dst me up);
And as the mirror of a lake
Yields back the lofty mountain's form,
So yields my thought the lovely shape,
Reflected of the vision bright.
Methought within yon cave I stood,
Pensive and shadowy was the light

Within the sacred place; alone
I stood beside the crystal stream,
And on its furtherest banks beheld,
On couch of fragrant moss reposed,
A sleeping maiden lie, with face
Upturned; a tender dreamy calm
Was on her brow, and o'er the mouth
And azured lids in slumber closed,
The faint sweet smiles rippled like light
Over a flowing brook; the hair
Lustrous and bright, in waves of gold
About the resting figure fell,
And half its dainty shape concealed:
Aurora's blushes on her cheek
Diffused; but the white virgin breast
Was as the lofty glacier's point
Unstained; but on that place of sweets
I planted not my lips, nor pressed
The ruby of her mouth; I knelt
And worshipped, but I touched her not,
She seemed too pure for mortal touch—
I knelt and worshipped."

      Without word
The queen arose and beckoned him
Toward the cave: softly they trod,
For an invisible spirit of awe

Hovered about the place. By dim
Uncertain light within disclosed,
It seemed a grotto large and fair;
The stalactites hung from the roof,
The crystal droppings of the rock.;
The turf beneath was smooth and soft
As richest velvet to the foot.
A bloom of roses lined the walls,
Young buds which turned toward the light
Scentless and pale. A rippling stream
Flowed through the cavern's length with sound
Subdued, and on the tranquil wave
A proud and stately lily lay
With petals waxy-white; above,
And round its orb of shining leaves,
A strain of mystic music rose,
As if an airy bird sang there
Unto the flower its chant of love,
(So sings the bulbul to the rose,
So sings the thrush to his young mate,
When 'neath the boughs she builds her nest;)
But bird was none; invisible
The mystic spirit trilled his notes
Of love, the angel of the flower
For ever hovering there.

                            With steps
Tender and slow the Prince approached,
" I see the vision of my dream
Renewed," he said, "even as the night
Revealed this place, I see it now.
The stuccoed roof, the gliding stream,
And the white lily on the wave
Reposed, the soft and mossy sward
With growth of roses wan and pale;
But she, the spirit of the place,
The fair and sleeping maid, who gave
All things their life and charm, and toned
Them all to beauty, where is she?
The loveliest shape that ever dawned
On the enraptured sight of man.
Without that presence sweet, nor life
Nor loveliness is here."

                            He spoke,
And the soft warbling bird-like notes
In silence died away; a hush
Ensued, and on his heart there crept
A sense of mystery and awe;
While slowly from the flower evolved
A pale and vapourous cloud, its folds
Like silvery mists round Dian's form
A bright and beauteous thing appeared

To wrap : softly the mist dissolved,
And the white purity it hid
Within its depths, stood forth revealed,
A lovely maiden to the sight.
Graceful her mien, a young sweet girl,
Scarce fifteen summers of the earth,
Had riped her downy cheek, or swelled
Her tender form to woman's port;
Moulded her fine and faultless limbs
Like the pure parian stone, by hand
Of genius wrought to shape divine;
And in her countenance the light
And radiant beauty of the soul
Shone forth in matchless loveliness!
Smiles played about the delicate lips,
And broke from out the willowy lash
Fringing those glorious azure eyes,
And nestled in the dimpled cheek.
Her hair in rippling waves of gold
Flowed o'er the white and swelling breast,
And draped her to the knee with veil
Of chastity. Timid and shy
She stood, and bent her meek regards
Upon the ground; thus stood, then turned,
Wavering irresolute, as she
Would flee, till by her lover's arm
Caught and detained, she paused, nor strove,

But on his manly breast let droop
Her hyacinthine head.

                        Then spoke
The majesty of the great deep—
"Take her, for she is thine; her wed,
And be the fruitage of your loves
For ever sweet. She as mine own
Among my children of the seas
Have I brought up, though human-born.
The orb of days, as men count time,
Two weeks of years have run since first
My beauteous one laid on my breast,
Drew the faint breath of infancy.
Beside the golden strand I walked
While with faint blushes in the east
Aurora rose, when o'er the beach
With thundering hoof one of my guards,
Returning from appointed watch,
Where ocean mingles with the earth
The boundary of his higher waves,
Came bearing on his saddle bows
A woman's pale and piteous corpse
From wreck received. This at my feet
He laid, while I bent o'er the dead
With sorrow traced the lineaments
Of loveliness not yet in death,

Effaced: the daughter of a king
She seemed, for the dank robes swathed
  round
Her limbs were such as royalty wears.
How beautiful was she! I stooped,
And weeping, kissed the fair cold clay,
Washed from a noble vessel's wreck,
My scout the lovely corpse to me
Had brought, noting its beauty; thus
I bent me weeping o'er the dead,
When 'neath my hand I felt the throb
Of life. Alas! sweet soul, she neared
The time of her maternity;
And in her cold imprisoning womb
She yet a living burden bore.
I from her ripped that hour the child,
And as mine own I nursed it at
My breast: though woman-born, it sucked
Of ocean-paps, as these the tribes
Native to the deep sea. It grew,
Within my halls, a peerless child.
Dandled on knees of ocean-powers,
Yea, by the mightiest nursed, so grew,
Happy and giving happiness;
My primest joy was she, and still
Increasing love to her I gave:
But when her fair sweet girlhood orbed

To early womanhood, the earth
By dim mysterious ties drew back
To her maternal breast her child.
Inly she pined, and oft the sighs
Unbidden came upon her lips;
She moved not in the dance, or moved
With languid steps; dreamy and sad,
Within this cave she loved to sit,
Dropping her slow and heavy tears
In quiet sadness on yon flower.
I saw, I pitied, I resolved,
Rending my heart to do her right,
I said, 'Go, pass into the flower,
The lily of sweet waters, thou
More pure shalt in her breast abide;
Sleep in thine innocence, and o'er
Thy rest mine holy ones shall keep
Perpetual watch.'

                Thee from the earth
I brought,—the noblest of her sons,—
Thy worth approved by many a test:
My purpose now I crown, and wake
From her enchanted sleep the fair
And dreaming maid ; a virgin pure
And uncontaminate she yields
Herself to thee : into thine arms

Messeria.

I give my child, though with her pass
The pearl, the treasure of my realm
Away, and leave me desolate."

      She turned,
And then, despite of regal pride,
Tears such as ocean-spirits shed,
Fell on the mossy sward.

      Yet spake
Once more the lady of the seas,
"Three times the moon must dip her horn
In the deep azure of mine heavens,
And rising as a crescent thrice,
Fulfil her circle in the sky,
Then shall ye to your native earth
Return; meanwhile be consummate
With holy rites your union pure:
I call th' assembly of my powers
To grace the proud hymeneal feast.
The monarchs of the deep shall come,
Not without gifts, and flight of nymphs
Shall sing you to your bridal rest."
She ceased, and from the cave went forth
Leaving the maiden at his side;
By his encircling arm enchained,
She, like the first pure bud of spring,

When the sweet breath of Heaven doth
    touch
With tender feel its opening leaves,
With tremulous emotion glowed.
Trembling and half abashed she stood,
Veiling her eyes beneath his gaze,
Then with a sudden impulse knelt,
And tossing back the clustered curls
From off her polished bow, gazed full
Into his face, while radiant smiles
Of tenderness broke from her lips;
Her brow, her cheek, her eyes, the light
And glory of a summer day.

*   *   *   *   *

Come, ye maidens of the deep,
Ye that haunt the ocean caves,
Dwellers 'neath the crystal waves,
Come and strike your sounding lyres.
Let the soul of music leap
Wild and free in notes of love.
Softer than the melting dove
Let your lingering voices fall
Gently on the raptured ear,
With a dying melody.
Then more loud, and then more clear,

Messeria.

With a sound like clarion call
Roll the mighty symphony.
Kindle all the mystic fires
In the slumberous heart that sleep,
Wake the boundless ecstacy
With a song of magic power,
In this happy nuptial hour.

They came, and with their fingers swept
Their harps of gold and wondrous lyres,
The music through the lofty halls
Resounded clear and long ; so sweet
It flooded with untold delight
The listener's breast, like the warm wind
That fills the heart of summer's rose,
Until the soul by its own love
Deflower'd, swooned in its bliss away.

The nuptial moon rose soft and clear;
Silver her light, and through the vales
Of ocean poured profuse, more bright
In honour of the bridal hour;
For she who ruled in those still realms
Did with her word control the powers
And elements of Nature there.
A fresher spring in those green vales
Opened its bosomed sweets, and gales

With odorous fanning wings diffused
The scents of cassia, nard, and balm.
The festive palace shone more bright,
And the great shapes of glowing light
That towered beside the colossal throne
Apparelled them in beauty; so
Came on the auspicious marriage hour.
Old ocean from his lair sent out
The dancing nymphs in glittering bands,
To hail the tender child of earth.
They shook their golden locks, and sang
Greetings and homage to the bride.

Then came she, blushing like the morn,
Ringed round with her attendant maids,
The changeful splendours o'er her face,
Chased like the fleeting April clouds;
And tender as the floral grace
Upon the meek-eyed April's breast
Her virgin beauties beamed, and bless'd
Serene th' admiring gazer's sight.
Lustrous her robe, and soft the veil
Down to the dainty feet that flowed
In airy and transparent folds.
To her th' enamoured bridegroom sprung,
And while the solemn nymphal rung
Through those high halls of ocean pride

Messeria.

By thousand, thousand sea-maids sung,
To her he pledged his constant vows
In words of feälty and truth.
Then spake the ocean queen, well pleased,
And blessed the marriage of the twain,
The auspicious union of the pure.

* * * * *

"Belovèd my soul's star! oh thou,
My beauteous lady, rise! arise
My love, my fair one, rise, behold
How calm, how beautiful the night!
She to her bowers invites us forth
With voice more sweet than Proserpine's,
Waking the flowers in vales of earth.
A fragrance drips upon the air,
And from the heart of silence sings
The nightingale a spousal hymn,
Delicious mystery of love,
Whose ecstasy thrills through each note
She pours! how calmly beautiful
The brooding soft tranquillity!
See, o'er the tops of yon tall trees
That skirt th' enchanted grove, the moon
Doth silvering rise, till higher yet
Ascending in the heavens, she throws

Her lustrous glory on the deep,
Where the adoring waters yield
Her image back: arise, my love,
My fairest, rise, and come with me."

She rose respondent to his call,
Alone and unattended, for
Attendants with them would they none;
Sole in their love and to themselves
Sufficient: silence enveloped them,
The holy stillness of the night,—
The purple dimness of the night,—
Love's meetest, softest robe.

       The vale
Upon her soft green lap shook out
Her fairest flowers, her buds profuse,
She opened for delight, and shed
The spicy fragrance of the pink
Upon the air. Hand linked in hand
They wandered through the shadowy groves
In trancèd dreamlike happiness.
Upon the laced and mazy paths
The moonbeam shot with quivering play,
Like to the tracery of light
Thrown on the chancel floor in old
And dim cathedrals: grand and sweet

The solemn splendour of its ray.
Within the sacred wood they came
Where fountains warbling flowed, and chimed
Perpetual music: from tree to tree
The vine her leafy foliage flung,
And trailing mosses lightly hung
From hoar and aged boughs on high;
While underfoot the velvet sward
Seemed, as the azure vault of Heaven,
Studded with stars, so thick inwrought
With living flowers of glorious hue.
Silent they went, as if they feared
By whispered word or sound to break
That spell of golden happiness.
The zephyr slept upon the flowers
Languid and faint, his wings oppressed
With heavy sweets, so lay his love
On hers, faint with its own excess.
Tender their steps and slow; so passed
They onward to the deepest bower
Of the enchanted wood, and there
On emerald bank they sat them down,
A couch more tender than the lap
Of May in all its flowery prime.
As in the secresy of woods
The female vine with spousal arms

Entwines the mighty oak, and coils
Her tendrils round its giant bulk,
So in her clasping soft embrace
The fair Messeria twined her lord,
Wreathing his neck with her white arms,
While on his breast she showered profuse
The golden glory of her hair.
Afar, in tufted darkness, sang
The nightingale, and faintly sweet
The droplets of the magic song
Flowed on the ear: but other sound
Was none. The dense enwoven shade
Of foliage thick above them spread,
Shook down its flowers upon their head;
But scarcely through the leafy screen
One tender moonbeam crept, so thick
Enwrapped in purple dimness seemed
That place, as consecrate to love,
A sacred nuptial bower.

* * * * *

                              Aloft
On throne of burnished gold she sat,
The lady of the ocean realms;
Around her ranged her ministers
Of state, the silver trumpets through

Her marble halls resounding clear
Proclaimed a synod of her powers.
Trooping they came, the great sea gods,
The nerëides and the nymphs
That at the helm of Neptune sit,
And guide with songs his green sea car;
The fairest Peris of his court,
The Oceanids, and dwellers of the deep,
From out their caves; obeisance made
And circled round her seat with songs
Of adoration; high she sate,
And from her regal brow diffused
Splendours around. Great rays of light,
Like brightness of the ascending sun
Kindling an alpine mount at dawn,
About her forehead flashed, and shone
Upon the host.

     "Powers of the sea,
First sceptres of the deep," she said,
"With allthe radiant phalanxes
That gird your greatness round, and you
The sisterhood of kingdoms sends
The fountain-haunting nymphs whom men
Call Naiädes, ye that in vales
Of earth the crispy marge of streams
Best love, witness ye all that this,

My son, with amplest heritage
I dower,   Lay at his feet your gifts,
The tribute offerings of the deep;
The pearls and tinted corals bring,
The scented amber from the shore,
With every precious gem that lies
Bedded in ocean's depths.   Ye nymphs
Of warbling fount and stream, that oft
With sedgy growth your locks entwine,
When to his native earth returned
He sways the sceptre of a realm,
The flowery pastures of his land
Your chosen habitations make;
Be there your favourite haunts recluse:
From out your urns pour on his fields
Changeless fertility; in time
Of drought, let there not lack to him
The rivulet of the mountain born,
Or azure sheeted lake, or pond
Of silver, where the sun and moon
And stars mirror themselves in beauty;
And you no less, ye twain great powers,
Supports of my imperial throne,
The prime incarnate essences
Of wind and wave,—him as your lord
Obey, and to him yoke submiss
Your powers; fill with thy favouring breath

His sails, thou greater of the twain;
To him in perfect gentleness
Appear; but on his enemies
Send thy most awful blasts.   And thou,
Oh woman, on thy swelling breast
His proud flotillas bear secure,
And with thy smooth lips kiss his prows
In sign of love."

                    So spake the Queen,
And through the vast assembly ran
Murmurs of approbation, low
And deep, like beatings of the wind
In caverned rocks beside the shore,
Which in a moment brake in sounds
Of glad acclaim, exultant shouts
Which rent the air: and the proud host
Of ocean-peers drew near the throne,
And on its golden steps laid down
Their gifts.   Trophies and gems more rich
The worshipping kings of earth ne'er gave
To him who sat on Israel's throne
In all his high and palmy state,
The world-famed ruler of the east.

        *   *   *   *   *

Messeria.

In chamber draped with hangings wove
By sea-nymphs in their wondrous looms,
With gold and opal tints inwrought,
And broideried o'er with gorgeous flowers,
Such as the garlands spring doth wear,
Ocænia sat, and at her feet
The children of her love, the Prince
And his young bride, she goodliest spouse
That e'er enriched the hand of man,
Sat pillowing on his knee her head;
Her fair dishevelled hair, half hid
The glowing crimson of her cheek,
And half in wreathen curls twined round
His arm; the tendrils of the vine
So coil embracive round the tree.
She from the forest glades had brought
Young flowers with morning's holiest dews
Impearled, in garlands wove to please
His eye; not without gift of fruits,
For 'mid the green and bowering leaves
The ruddy fruitage freshly glowed;
He for the lovely giver's sake
The lovely gift received, but scarce
The luscious offering won regard
While her more luscious beauties charmed,
More sweet, more pure than those young
    buds

In which the tender dewdrops swelled,
Or those rich fruits in all their bloom,
Clustered amid the leaves. Oft through
The willowy fringes of her eye
The young wife stole a timid glance
To mark his brow, until her looks
Fell 'neath his gaze, meekly abashed.
Thus sat they, and the soft sweet flow
Of talk was tender as the brook
Of summer, when it rippling runs
Through sylvan shades in leafy woods
In hush of dreamy solitude.
Through the closed doors the sounds of song
And music came, subdued and low,
In interchange of amorous strains
And solemn tunes, or sweet or wild.
The ocean-nymphs within the halls
Rejoicing, touched their harps, and poured
The high melodious song. They sat
With hands enlocked, while o'er them bent
The stately Queen, and in their joy
Rejoiced ; when failed the tender talk,
Silence than words more eloquent
Their hearts meetly expressed : so flowed
The time along—moments of bliss—
Till on the youthful husband's brow

An evanescent sadness gathered,
Like to the cloud of April, when
It falls its fruitful drops, while yet
The glory of his beams the sun
Veils not. "My love, my wife," he said,
"Three days have slid in bliss away,
And I from thee have scarcely loosed,
Happy round thee to twine, and lock
More close, the tendrils of embrace:
Now for a moment from thy side,
Must I depart, my sweet, and breathe
Apart,—from my felicity!
For strong upon my heart is come
A longing masterless and great:
I faint to hear my father's voice;
To see once more the face of her
Who bare me,—she who was my star
Of infancy—parent most dear.
For one brief hour I visit earth,
And thence will come to thee and bring
Upon my heart its chastity
Unsmirched. I go, but tarry not;
Swift shall my journey be, and brief,
Pauseless: I will not taste of bread,
Nor shall the juices of the grape
Moisten my lip, till I again
Behold thy face."

He spoke, and pressed
Her lily hands close to his breast,
Gathering by touch ineffable
The sweetness of her presence sweet.
"My mother and my Queen," he said,
"My sovereign lady, speak consent."
He to Ocænia turned and made
Request, but she gave not reply.
The great sublimity stood silent,
Clouding her brow with quiet grief,
Nor spoke until the second time
He plied his quest. "My son," she said,
"Your will is free; behold, my gates
Stand open, and my cohorts wait
To guard you on your way: the sea
At my command shall ope her doors
And give you passage to the earth;
Go then, but be your vow observed."

Weeping, he kissed his weeping bride,
And gently from his neck unwound
Her clinging arms, and then with head
Over his shoulder turned, and eyes
Which to the last did bend on her
Their stedfast sad regards, he left
The ocean-halls, and took his way
From thence, like one lost in a dream.

PART IV.

Where the dark flood laves with its waves
The desolate shore, there is a wood,
A forest large, and dank and drear,
Flowerless, and fruitless; coldly there
The wintry sun sheds his cold beams;
The sad funereal cypress glooms;
The poplar and the sombrous pine
Darken the paths, and 'neath their shade,
Pale, leaden grey, the dull pools sleep
In many a haunted dell: the wind,
With sound like wail of human pain,
Moans through the quivering forest boughs.
Erie and sad. With bleeding feet,
And head uncovered to the blast,
A woman wanders there; her form
Is bowed, her eyes are dim with tears;
Yet never beauty wore in joy
Such charm as her soft pensive grace.
The lily of the seas, the white
Unspotted flower, what does she here
In this most desolate place? the pride
Of ocean cast upon the earth
In poverty and woe.

Messeria.

    Long, long
She waited in her regal home
The coming of her lord. Long, long
She waited while the mournful days
Went slowly by, but he came not.
Now on the borders of his land
She strays, and like the bird that flits,
Wailing around its ravaged nest,
Weeping, she hovers near the place
Of his abode. Patient and true,
Through tedious time had she kept watch;
She could not frame one thought of guile,
And e'en in dreams, her constant heart
Did image only his return.
Full of meek hope she waited him,
And twined each day her golden locks
With coronal of fresh green leaves,
And decked in dainty robes her form
To meet his eye with added charms.
Through the long night she trimmed the lamp
That in her turret window shone,
That he might catch its beams afar;
Or on the craggy rock she sat,
Straining her gaze across the flood
Through the still watches of the night,
Till on the waters flamed the dawn.

But he came not; in vain, in vain,
Her patient tryst, yet sweetly meek
Her soul retained its faith; and she,
In ocean's inmost groves had decked
A bower with fairest flowers, the rare
And virgin flora of the woods,
She, from its hiding places, brought
And planted for adornment there:
And she had taught the rose to climb
And shed her petals from on high,
And drawn more close the drapery
Of boughs, which screened the lovely place,
There oft at eve she pensive sat
And woke the softly warbling flute.
Lulling her soul with gentle sounds,
Until her tears flowed o'er her cheek,
But he to her returned no more.
Thus in her sylvan bower she sat
One dewy eve, while winds were hushed,
When moved the shadowy boughs aside,
Appeared a form of light, a nymph,
" With flower-inwoven tresses torn;"
Lovely her face, although in woe,
And to her robe of gossamer,
With dew bespangled o'er, yet clung
The briars of the wilderness,
As she in haste had travelled far.

Low at Messeria's feet she knelt;
And as she kissed her garment's hem,
Thus spoke—"Dear lady, from the earth
I come; amid the falling spray
Of a fair fountain in the halls
Of his ancestral home, whom late
Our most dread sovereign named her son,
Thy husband best beloved, I make
Abode, a naiad of the fount.
There, 'mong the lotus on the wave
That rock, I couch or lightly dance;
Myself invisible, save when
From out the silvery spray I rise
On mortal sight of mine own will,
Lady—sweet flower of earth."—She turned,
And more she would have said, but lost
Her voice in weeping. Wonderingly
Messeria heard; quick to her cheek
Had flushed the crimson tide, as quick
Rebounded to her heart; her face
Waxed wan and cold, and scarce her lips
Obeyed to shape her words—"Lives he,
And is he well, my most dear lord?"
She said. "Say, hast thou seen his face?"
The naiad answered, "He is well.
Lady—sweet one—for thee I weep!
I saw the princely youth's return,

When 'mid the admiring throng he stood
Like a new-lighted god! His sire,
Who as the full-eared corn was weighed
With days and honours, clasped his son
Rejoicing, nor exulted less
His mother, as she anchoring hung
Upon his neck, and gave him greetings.
'Behold!' the aged monarch said,
'Behold, mine head is white with age;
To thee, my son, will I resign
The weight of sovereingty: be thine
Henceforth the sceptre and the throne.'
Much of the past they questioned him;
But of the secrets of the deep
Forbid to speak, he gave but scant
Reply. Brief time he tarried; then,
All weeping, tore himself from out
His mother's arms, and spoke adieus.
'Stay, stay,' they cried, 'the night comes on!
But if thou wilt not stay, yet taste
Of food ere thou depart!'

"From out
The weeping waters, where I dwell,
I saw a handmaid of the queen
Approach; she raised the chaliced cup:
I saw the sparkling wine o'erflow.

Graceful as Hebè when she tends
The reposing gods in heavenly feast,
She tendered the alluring draught.
Thrice he refused, thrice made denial;
But she, with soft persuasion, still
Enticed; his lips were wan, his throat
Was dry: by faint oppressive thirst
O'ercome, he yielded slow consent.
He took the bowl, he quaffed deep draughts,
And laughter leapt upon his lips!
And from that moment seemed to fade
Like print of a forgotten dream,
All memory of the past from out
His mind. Contented he abode,
And fixed his home in those proud halls,
Th' anointed sovereign of the realm
Is he. Among the great of earth
He builds himself a name; and she,
The proud and courtly maid they name
His bride."

     She ceased, and bent her eyes
Upon the ground, silent and sad,
Then like a cloud of silvery spray
She showed among the enwreathing boughs,
And, as the floating mist of morn,
She faded from Messeria's sight.

Cold drops fell on her hands and face
Like tears of pity; and even thus
The weeping naiad passed away.

So came the lily of the seas
To earth, and thus amid the shades
Of the dank wood she made abode.
Single, alone; for of the tribes
Of Ocean would she take no nymph
To tend her steps.   Alone she sought
Her lord, if haply she might win
Once more his smile; and she had put
The raiment of her glory off,
And clad herself in lowly garb;
But the mean weeds were unto her
Like the thin sculptured drapery
Of antique statue, which reveals—
Not hides—its majesty of form.
Her hair no more in ringlets shed
To frolic with each loving breeze,
In heavy plaits around her head
She coiled, a simple austere charm.
With weary step she paced the wood.
The berries harsh, and harsher roots,
To her were food, and from the spring
She drank; yet from her gentle lips
No murmur slid.   And in that place

Messeria.

Nature did faintly own the touch
Of her sweet womanhood. Lo! where
She couched at night, at dawn appeared
Young flowers; the delicate primrose reared
Its pale gold crest, to fall, alas!
Too soon before the northern blast.
With her there came a milk-white bird,
Stainless its plumage, purer than
The riven snow, by foot unpressed;
It sung not, but it lay within
Her breast, nestled, and kept it warm.

The chilly spring came sadly on,
Not in ethereal mildness now
Descending on the mead, while wakes
Th' ambrosial freshness round; but wan
And dank with ceaseless showers, pale, grey,
And cold. The spring-tide growths shot forth
Fragile and weak, with quivering leaf.
The young plants, by the sun unkissed,
Died in their cold virginity,
And bore no flower. More faint, more wan
The buds of hope in that young heart,
Struck by a blast, more fierce, more cruel,
They drooped with beauties all unoped.

* * * *

She slept within a forest copse;
The tall and plumy ferns enclosed
The spot, and tangled its approach,
While from above the willow drooped
Its boughs; the pensive light of dawn
Played on her marble brow, and o'er
The swollen and violet-coloured lids
A wannish lustre shed; slow tears
Trickled from 'neath the fringy lash
And hung upon the downy cheek.
One fair white hand passed 'neath her head,
The other on her breast reposed,
Listless and nerveless: thus she lay,
And in her dreams her sweet lips shaped
The name for ever loved.
      She woke
From slumber, and behold, was there
Close at her bare uncovered breast,
A serpent raised, in act to strike.
But when the reptile met the gaze
Of those soft eyes, it crouched to earth,
And licked the ground before her feet,
Fawning; while all around, above,
Beneath, aërial music seemed
To rise and swell upon the gale,
In melting notes prolonged and sweet.
It ceased, the soft mysterious sound;

Silence renewed itself, more still;
The morn was sad, but sadder far
The young wife's heart, yet strangely calmed,
It seemed as if that mystic strain
Had steeled her soul with purpose high,
And she arose in that same hour,
Girded herself, and set her face
Toward the palace of her lord.

* * * *

The festal lights in the high halls
Are kindled, and the guests are there,
Princes and knights high-famed, but chief
And centre of all eyes, is she,
The stately lady, whom they name,
The youthful sovereign's bride. He moves
Among th' assembled guests, with front
Lofty and proud, yet oft his eye
Stoops to the ground, or idly sweeps
The bannered walls as though he sought,
Something, he knew not what. The fair
And courtly maiden at his side
Upon her royal lover smiles,
Yet fixes not his wavering eye.

Hither, from out her forest lair,

In lowly garb Messeria came.
She stood amid the menial throng,
And as a servant in the halls
Of her great lord, she served his guest,
Humbling herself, that she might see
Once more his face.   With her she brought,
Hid 'neath the foldings of her vest,
The bird of stainless wing; it lay
Songless and mute within her breast,
Rocked by the beating of her heart.
She saw once more the face of him
She loved; and her dilated eye
Did for a moment drink its fill
Of bliss; forgetful of all woe,
Her soul quaffed the ecstatic draught
Intoxicate with strange delight;
Then, with a shuddering sigh, more sad,
She drooped in lonely widowhood
Of heart.

    The feast is set, the wine
In golden goblet brims, but hark!
What soft melodious sounds are these
Slow floating through the vaulted halls?
More sweet, more soft th' æolian harp,
In leafy woods touched by the wind,
Breathes not its notes.   Like beam of light

The white-wing'd bird speeds through the halls;
It soars, it sings—so sings the lark,
And at the gates of morn upsprings.
Yet not as lark that mystic bird
Trills its melodious notes. Three times
In eddying flight it swept around,
Then rested on the young king's hand,
Nestled and seemed to woo caress.
He, with the tender movement pleased,
Stroked the meek thing and smoothed its crest,
Strange dim emotions seemed to stir
His soul; he trembled, and was touched!
Then came Messeria near; she crept
With noiseless step close to his side,
Covered her face and knelt before him.
He o'er her stooped, and gently raised
The sable coiffure from her head,
And the pale glory of the hair,
Which saint-like haloed round her brow,
Unveiled—"My husband and my lord!"
Brake from her lips, "My wife!" from his,
Nor more they spoke, but locked in close
Embrace, while on her low-bowed head,
Pillowed upon his throbbing breast,
The great tears fell like heavy rain.

Weeping, they thus together clung;
Silent long time, heart pressed to heart:
Then raised he up her face and gazed
Fondly and long thereon, while from
His lips, his eyes, he shed on her
Sunshine of smiles. So the sweet rays
From opening eyelids of the morn
Fall on the flowers. Enamoured thus,
He hung o'er his recovered wife,
Forgetful of all presence there,
Thus for awhile; then lifted he
His kingly brow, and unto those
Who stood around—knights of his court—
He told in simple words, and brief,
The story of his love; how he
Had woo'd and won the Ocean-maid.
Yet after, from him cast the flower,
The stainless lily of the seas,
Not wisting what he did. Then turned,
And unto them, his ministers,
Who waited round the däis steps,
Thus spoke, "Bring ye the diadem,
The golden circlet of the realm,
And set it on her brow." They heard,
Obeyed. Flashing with gems, and wrought
With work of subtlest jewelry,
Handed from kings of ancient time,

They placed the symbol on her head.
Upon the lustrous braids of hair
It sat—a glory on a glory.
She by her kingly husband stood,
Queenliest of queens, for she was fair
Beyond all women of the earth!
Goodly they deemed her, who beheld,
And the great peers with low-bowed knee
Worshipped, and unto the fair queen
Gave homage. All around was joy,
And on all faces radiant smiles,
Worthy the nuptials of a king.

To a Butterfly.

  Come, rest by me,
With gilded wing upon the flower,
And charm me for one fleeting hour!
  Come, rest by me,
And make me joyful with the sight
Of an embodied beam of light!
  Dear child of spring!
Sweet April's fairest darling thou,
That gently flutterest round her brow,
  When from her heart
Goes up through leaf and bud above,
The first faint thrill of virgin love!
  Thou frailest thing
That nature has, how fair thou art,
And yet of strength how small thy part!
  One touch of mine
Would brush the beauty from thy wing,
And unto dust thy glory bring!
  Great Nature's child,
Go sport upon the mother's breast!
But for a moment is thy rest.

To a Butterfly.

I own,—I feel
A life whose vast immensity
Ages unroll: and yet there be
    Some ties which bind
My soul to thee, thou trembling thing.
And there be thoughts untold that bring—
    Tremblingly bring
The tear-drops to mine eyes: sweet thought
And tender memory are brought
    Of days long past,
The joy and sorrow of a dream
With thy bright flickering gleam.
    Creature so frail,
I, that am human, own with thee
Some links of sympathy: to me,
    Sweet wanderer,
Thou art no insect, but a light
From out the past, tender and bright!

The Naiad.

    THE willows dipped
Their hoary branches in the dark blue waters;
The breath of summer's night slept on the
  face
Of the reposing lake, embosomed deep
Within an antique wood, where knotted trees,
Enormous growth of centuries,—piled o'er-
  head
A massive roof of boughs,—inwoven shade!—
Through vistas long outstretched; sombre
  and grand,
Through the dim forest aisles, mysterious
  awe
And silence crept, as if invisible.
The spirit of great Nature there abode,
And with mysterious rites was celebrated.
The willows dipped them in the dark blue
  waves,
Where floating lilies lay, white, cold, and
  pure.
Upon the centre of the 'sleeping lake
Shone the reflection of the silver moon,

The moon and stars! another Heaven below,
More immaterial, more spiritual
In beauty, if that might be, than that above!
Where the pale glory lay, the waters flowed
Apart, and thence emerged a lovely form,
Pale as the splendour out of which she rose,
A Naiad sprang, uplift above the wave,
White as the stainless lilies round her couched
Her breast of snow and gleaming arms; the head
Was diademmed with flowers which seemed to wear
The moon's soft lustre on their petals pure.
And in the dark and lustrous hair which flowed
All wet upon the shoulders fair, pale pearls
Gleamed like the dew-drops on the locks of night.
The face, serenely calm and sweet, a strange
And solemn beauty wore, and in the eyes
Uplifted, the rapt soul adoring sat.
Ne'er saw or dreamed I face so beautiful,
Or splendour shaded so with tenderness;
Like great angelic glories dimmed with awe
And gentlest love! or as the dim rich light
Softly through old Cathedral windows shed,

With glory-shapes and gorgeous colours
    dight.
Such might she be who rose in Milton's
    thoughts,
Vision of divinest melancholy.
She seemed the spirit of the hour and place:
Incarnate beauty born of holiest peace.
A vestal from the heart of nature risen
To be the symbol of the silent worship
In that great forest-temple offered up.
The hands upon the breast were crossed;
    the head
Bowed down, low to the wave she bent her
    down
And passed from sight. So the bright
    vision ceased;
It passed and was no more.

May.

Come with me, love, a-Maying!
Come ere the bees are playing;
Come while the dew is lying,
And cloud with cloud is vying,
   And lightly floating by
   In the soft morning sky.
   Come to the flowery mead,
   Where the sweet pleasures lead
The airy dance and mirthful song,
For ever fair and ever young;
    Come, love, with me!

Sit with me, love, a-Maying,
'Neath the white branches swaying,
Where the young violet, dying,
Sends out her soul in sighing,
   And breathes of nought but love
   To the rapt breeze above.
   Here on a flowery bed
   Mine heart to thine I'd wed,
And all the sweetness of the May
Pour out in many a tender lay,
    My love, to thee!

The Cup of Tears.

The child was young and fair,
Soft its eyes and bright its hair,
But sickness on it lay,
And the little one passed away.
The mother she wept in her grief,
Disconsolate without relief,
Day and night wept she,—night and day.
It was midnight, and there rose,
In the chamber small and dim,
Where no fire nor lamp-light glows,
With sound of music mild
The semblance of a child,
A visionary babe—
Lovely angel of the Lord,
Such as those who wait His word,
And soft before Him wave
Fragrant censers of their praise,
While a ceaseless song they raise.
Tender looks of love it wore,
In its hand a cup it bore,
Full was it unto the brim,
Filled unto the topmost rim.

The Cup of Tears.

The midnight air was riven
With the voice so soft and clear,
Thus it spoke, the vision bright,—
"From the angelic bower,
Where nestling cherubs sleep
Beneath the wings that keep
In shelter close and deep
The little ones of heaven,
In this sweet and solemn hour
Come I to thee, my mother dear.
Lo! the sorrow-cup I bear,
In it gathered every tear
Weeping thou for me hast shed:
If the cup should overflow,
Though among the saints I glow,
And the heavenly dances tread,
Must I taste of mortal woe,
And in mourning bow me low!"
Thus it spoke, then passed from sight,
The lovely child of light.

And the mother wept no more;
   Hushed she for her darling's sake
All her grief so great and sore
   Lest the little one partake.

To the Violet.

MEEKEST of things, thou soul of lowly love,
That hid'st thyself and giv'st thy sweetness
 forth!
There be like thee that in the dimness dwell,
Sweet souls, that in them hold the breath of
 Heaven,
And give to human hearts the life divine
In them condensed. Meek flower that in
 the shade
Dost like a virgin hide, and make thine
 home;
Thee the wind woos, and the soft dews of
 morn
Do visit thee with benediction pure;
And unto thee is given the love of men
In measure large and full, the fond regards
Of children, and the poet's ripest praise.
Thy sister, the white lily of the vale,
Is not to men more dear than thou, a thing
Of vestal purity; to us she speaks
Of chastity unsmirched, but thou of love,
Tender humility, and all sweet grace.

The Echo.

Know you where the echo dwells?
   Spirit of mysterious sound,
In a cave where waters fall
   Gurgling, dashing, sweeping round,
'Neath great walls of pendant rock,
   Her with joy I lately found,
Maiden wild with streaming hair,
   Gleaming, glancing, glittering eye,
Maiden wild and yet most fair.
As laughing loud I made approach,
   Loud she laughed and hid her there.
When I woo'd her with soft words,
   Mockingly she made reply;
Distant was her voice and low,
   Distant, faint, and then seemed nigh.
A thousand thousand tongues in one,
   A thousand thousand mystic tongues.
When a mournful note I trill'd,
   Mournful too she chimed her songs,
Mystic-sad as angel's grief,
   Such note to heavenly grief belongs—
Melodious, tender, wild, and sweet.

The Echo.

With a faint and dying fall
Flowed her voice upon the ear,
  Sound of wonder to enthrall.
Maiden of the lonely soul,
  Secret, shy, and most retired,
Speaking from her darksome grot,
  Like a sybil voice inspired,
Prophet voice of one of old.
  Dreaming I beheld her face,
Saw her fill the darksome place,
  With an overflowing grace.

An Evening Vision.

A SINGLE star was in the west,
Serene and pure, the evening's gem.
Above the solitary splendour
Sailed through the cloudless sapphire depths
The crescent moon, her silver horns
Just deepening into gold. With heart
Of breathless awe all nature stood ;
The beauty of the heaven was on
The earth: its deep tranquillity,
Its holy calm, so hushed, so still,
It was as if the great earth bowed
In silent prayer. Across the horns
Of the pale moon, dimly revealed
A youthful Dian lay—a fair
And sleeping maid ;—her resting arm
Pillowed her head, upon her face
A rapturous beauty of repose
Was shed ; and round the mouth and eyes
In slumber closed, a faint light played,
Like the first glimmerings of a joy
Before it ripples into smiles.

The light robe from her form was thrown,
In guileless innocence she lay,
Her white limbs, pure as sculptured stone,
Ineffable in loveliness
Appeared.   So exquisitely fair,
So delicately sweet, unstained
And pure the lovely vision beamed.
No nymphs sustained her silvery car,
Or floated with her through the air:
Attendants she had none, nor was
There need of them,—the heavenly maid
Was all in all.   The very air
Was flooded with her presence sweet,
The wind entranced was still, the leaves
Upon the trees did scarcely move,
The river flowed with murmurs soft.

Oh glorious vision, passing sweet!
Oh holiness of unveiled beauty!
Oh ecstacy of perfect rest!

I had been sad, but at the sight
Thereof there came upon my soul
A kindred peace and purity,
A hush of deep serenity.
Then knew I what the old Greeks saw
When worshipping the virgin goddess,

They idealized the purity
Of nature, that deep sanctity
On which no stain hath ever come,
Or ever shall. Oh! heavenly maid,
Daughter of God, for ever thou
Abidest thus, and in the heart
Of nature mak'st thine holy rest.

The Girl at the Fountain.

A GLEAMING spring beside a mountain—
   Its waters leaping wild and sweet;
A dreamy maiden by the fountain—
   A village maid with naked feet.
The shadows o'er the grass are gliding,
   The tender shades of passing day;
The pitcher from her hand is sliding,
   But she, in thought, is far away.
The half-veiled bosom softly heaves,
   As freighted with some gentle pleasure;
A lovelier charm the dimple weaves,
   Coyed in her cheek with all its treasure.
Beautiful eyes, in whose soft night
Abides a vision of delight!
Beautiful lips, so sweetly smiling,
Although no gazer's heart beguiling.
The foaming waters lave her feet,
But scarcely are more white than they.
The bending branches graceful sway
In radiance of the passing day.
     More graceful is her form,
     With light and lithsome charm,

    More lovely is her face,
   Where all sweet beauties meet
    With soft and tender grace.
So crystal clear the fountain springs
In all its pristine purity,
You to its utmost depths may see,
As high its foamy flakes it flings.
As crystal clear her guileless heart,
As sweet the thoughts with which it rings,
While to her face the splendours start,
And touch her cheek with dimpled glee,
Yet to its depths I cannot see;
And at those thoughts I cannot guess,
To track their secrets more or less.
    But be they what they may,
   I know that light on angel wings
    Is not more pure than they.

To a Cuckoo.

Oh welcome! welcome to our land,
      Thou spiritual thing!
As silent here I trancèd stand,
      I hear Thy voice
As from a heart of mystery,
      Ringing soft and clear,
Distant, faintly, then more near,
      Floating on the air!
A sweet and artless melody,
      Two notes—no more.
Oh welcome! welcome! and more dear
      Than flowers to spring
Thou Bird unseen! I hear Thy voice
      From out the woods,
Or dropping from a cloud on high,
      As Thou floatest by.
Through the broad ethereal sky,
      Strangely, sweetly comes
The sound—I hear it and rejoice!

The Child Christ.

Shed on our hearts Thy meekness, Thou
    child Christ,
The consecration sweet of that fair image
Which filled the heart of ages past with
    beauty,
Till art enshrined it in her holiest place,
And made the temple of the beautiful
More beautiful—divine! Lowly to-day
Our proud hearts stoop, to Thee thou lowly
    child,
And reverently adore! Yet it may be,
Thou tender babe upon the mother's breast,
Thine was a place of glory in the realms
Of God, that mounting seraphs, when they
    climb
The steep ascents of fire, yet fail to reach.

Even for the lily and the violet,
And for the white and crimson rose, the
    rose
Wrapped in her modesty of mantling moss,

For these fair flowers, the lovely birth of
   earth,
And for our fairer human flowers, young
   babes
And children undefiled, for these to God
We tender thanks; for in them we behold
The wondrous beauty of the eternal mind
As in a mirror glassed. Then how much
   more
For Thee, Thou glory-flower of human
   things,
Himself incarnate in a child.

The Harvest Moon.

The moon rose from behind a hill
Full orbed—the large and golden harvest moon:
Around her all the sky, pale lavender,
Appeared, as with her soft and burnished beams
Just tinged with gold, the shadowings of her skirt
Of glory—so she rose beauteous and fair,
And seemed another sun, but shorn in part
Of his resplendent light and warmth. She rose
And looked upon the fields of ripened grain,
Dewy with evening's tears, as if she shed
A benison of peace with those bright beams;
The pale and silvery Dian changed and flushed
Seemed as a mother blessing the quiet earth
In her maternal love!

Rosa May.

Pretty Rosa May,
Merry, laughing, fay,
She hath birdies two,
Little pets so true:
Them she holdeth dear,
Ever keeps them near;
On her gentle breast
Gives the birdies rest.

Pretty Rosa May,
Sweeter than the day;
She hath suitors two,
Tender, fond, and true;
Them she holds not dear,
Never calls them near,
On her gentle breast
Gives them not to rest.

The Primrose.

KNOW you where the primrose hides?
She, my lady soft and fair,
Couchèd in her lonely lair.
In a solitary place,
There she dwells and she abides,
Shedding round a winsome grace;
Though the blustering winds be rough
Where the tender sunbeam creeps
And woos the maiden floweret forth,
Kissing her while yet she sleeps
In the hoary winter's lap.
Wandering in such place by hap,
Lately I with joy espied
Her white purity of face,
Gleaming like a star of light
On the pale high brow of night;
Her faint mystical perfume,
Softly, sweetly on me stole,
And I said—It is enough;
Thee, gentle flower, do I prefer,
Before the floral tribes of spring—
Thee, chiefly of the train I sing,
And to thee my homage bring.

The Primrose.

Sweet! to me do thou unroll,
While I tarry at thy side,
All the beauty of thy soul,
All thy inner mystery.
Gentlest, loveliest, tenderest birth,
Of the spring interpreter,
When she rises from her tomb
In the hoary, frozen earth,
Thou shalt be elect of flowers to me!

The Pixie Dance.

A POOL within an old grey wood,
A spectral pale and leaden sky,
Through the dank boughs the shuddering wind
Did creep, and slow into the sky
The wan and ghostly moon climbed up
Behind a veil of vapoury mist;
The pendant willows by the lake
Dipped them within the waters cold,
And hoary boughs of aged trees,
That grew beside the dreary tarn,
Spread out fantastic giant arms
Above the dark and solemn wave,
A weird and mystic shade. Remote.
Within the tufted grove, the bird
Of night sent forth his boding cry,
A melancholy note, which dropped
Upon the stillness of the hour
Demoniac, wild and strange. A place
It seemed, where nature rose in darkness,
With incantations on her lips,
And awful spells.

The Pixie Dance.

                With sound more soft
Than feather wafted from the wing
Of bird that soars on high, came down
Upon the silent pool a host
Of small white forms, creatures that danced
Like motes i' the sunbeam, countless and
    small.
They slid them down upon the air
Without a sound. And as they came
The moon broke from her vapoury folds
And changed her face to brightness. Soft
And sweet the night wind breathed, and
    voice
Was heard of grasshopper, that chirped
Upon the water's grassy marge.
With nimble feet they skimmed the lake
In circlets, o'er its breast they danced,
In many a wanton mazy round ;
With linkèd hands and mystic song,
Aërial music, wild and sweet,
Such notes as seemed not of the earth,
Nor scarcely of the heavens.

                      Sad, soft
And sweet, the tiny people raised
Their song—a spirit melody—
Which from the heart of midnight rang,

Countless and small, and bright were they,
And in their arms they changelings bore,
Which often in the wave they dipped,
To make immortal as themselves.
They sometimes on the shadowy green,
Beneath the pale and midnight moon,
Their charmèd elfin circlets draw;
Or o'er the dim and marshy moor,
In semblance of a wandering fire,
The 'lated traveller lure; or in
The dewy breast of opening buds
Couch they the livelong night, and suck
The honey sweets; but now their sport
Was here. A host of tiny things,
They came with mirth and revelry.
Upon the skirts of darkness hang
They evermore the elves of night,
The souls of unbaptizèd babes—
The night receives them to her breast,
And gives them tendence and delight.

The Lily of the Vale.

I saw in dreams young cherubs stand
About the feet of God; their wings were white,
Their wings were bright, and round about them shed
Ambrosial sweets! The heavenly Father spoke
In accents clear and loud; through heaven His voice
Was heard, "Which of my children, pure and white,
Will go for me to earth? Among my bands
Of radiant saints in this fair Paradise,
Where shall I find my meetest messenger
To bear to earth, and on her breast diffuse
The fragrance and the purity of this
Mine holy dwelling place?"

                        Then saw I stand
Before His face, a cherub mild and fair,
More lovely than a child of earth, but like
To such it seemed—a fair and female child.

"Father, I go," she whispering spoke, then
  bowed
And veiled her with her lovely wings, more
  pure,
More sweet than petals of the lily flower.
I saw the moving of a thousand wings,
And far and wide the glory-fields of heaven
Were filled with breath of odours rich.
                              Such was
My dream; its meaning then I did not know,
Nor scarcely know I now.

*   *   *   *   *

                              It was the spring,
And the bare earth was flushing with the
  feel
Of life new-born, when in a vale I stood,
And with delicious joy, low at my feet
Beheld a lily 'mid her clustering leaves,
Seated in queenly grace. She from the
  sight
Did half withhold her beauty, half revealed,
Half hid amid those green and shining
  leaves.
Looking on her, I seemed to see again
The vision of my dream, the face of God,

And the white angel standing at His feet,
And all the fragrance of the heavenly fields
Renewed itself that hour. I hailed and blessed
The lovely grace, the maiden of my dream,
The incarnate cherub in the flower.

The Birds.

COME to me, come to me, sweet!
Underneath the green boughs
I have found me a place, a place for our nest,
Secret and sheltered and meet,
The tall tree allows,
A leafy green bower, a fit place for our rest.
Come with wing rapid and fleet,
I will chant to thee vows,
I will sing to thee, dearest, sweet songs, tender songs,
Meltingly, meltingly soft,
In the bright summer day.
I will sing of the joy, the joy in my heart,
Till mounting, mounting aloft,
I will wing me away
To the far teeming fields, to find the sweet food
Our little ones ask for,
Our wee little birds.

In the beautiful nest beneath the green
   boughs,
      Sweetly and soft I will pour
      The glad song—the words
Of our wonderful joy, in wild music trilled.

To a Child.

WHAT is like thee, little child?
    What is like thee, darling mine?
Dappled fawn from out the woods,
    Eyes so dark, and soft, and fine;
Lark that sings in highest heaven,
    Soaring, floating, pouring songs,
Soul of fire in sweetness given:
    Rose that blooms in secret bower,
Scattering sweets upon the breeze,
    Bathed in dew the lovely flower:
Dove that nestles in the breast,
    Moveless, stirless, as the air,
Folded wings and heart at rest:
    Bee that sucks the honey flowers,
Sporting, toying, with the buds,
    Through the summer golden hours.
These are not so sweet as thou,
    Dainty child with eyes so bright,
Laughing lips and sunny brow,
    Dancing, sparkling like the foam,
Like the flakes on ocean's breast,

To a Child.

Making glad a happy home,
With thy guileless winsome ways,
Ceaseless source of pure delight,
Through the long and lingering days.

To the Primrose.

Come, gentle stranger, come,
The pale-faced daughter of the year,
   The tenderest birth of Spring;
Come, gentle flower, your beauties wear!

   The wintry cold is past,
The rain is gone, the wind is hushed,
   The sun is in the heaven,
And from its face the clouds are brushed.

   Love of my childhood's days,
How often have I welcomed thee?
   How joyed in mead and wood,
And sunny place thy face to see!

   I greet thee as I did,
I love to hail thy star-like light,
   In shadiest covert hid,
Where dawn with thee the violets bright.

   I love within the wood,
Upon the hill, beside the stream,
   Upon the barren spot,
To track thy soft and tender beam.

To the Primrose.

Thou thing of paly gold,
I love to see thy faint sweet sheen,
   So delicately pure,
Embowered 'mid leaves of softest green.

   I kiss thy tender lips,
As in the happy days gone by;
   Thou art to me, a dim
Mysterious joy, I know not why.

   Ah! joy so sweet, so wild,
The vanished years come back to me,
   I am again a child,
While, gentle flower, I gaze on thee.

The Naiad.

BESIDE a fountain dreaming
   I strayed one summer's day,
And in the water gleaming,
   Bright as the sunny May
Upon the green earth beaming,
   Behold a Naiad lay,
Her hair around her streaming
   In wildest disarray.
She shone in lovely seeming,
   Dim, sweet, and far away,
Down in the crystal sleeping,
   The maiden of the fount,
Bright in the sun upleaping,
   Whose waters, as they mount,
Fresh sweetness round her keeping,
   Do ever as I count
Rich showers of blessing weeping,
   The spirit of the fount
Express, serenely in it, sleeping.

Alice.

SAY, do you love me?
Whisper it soft, Alice, love of my heart,
  Coy and so sweet!
Gentle white bosom, your secrets impart.
  Rosy red mouth,
Kisses so sweet, will you tell me the tale?
  Love kindles love;
Dearly I love you; say, how can I fail?
  Little white hands,
Snowy fair, snowy soft, fingers so fine,
  Weave them in mine,
Link them in fondly, my darling, with mine.
  Dewy eyes drooping,
Sweet musings hiding, to what do they tend?
  Lily-fair form,
Slenderly beautiful, tenderly bend,
  Rest on my breast,
Trustingly, yieldingly, make it your nest.
  Soft as a bird,
Nestle you, nestle you, make it your rest.

To the Snowdrop.

BEFORE the first red buds of spring unfold,
Or cuckoo's voice is heard, thy face is seen,
    Flower of the winter, hail!
    Thou wee sweet darling, hail!

Sweeter to me than April's opening buds,
Or flowers and scented blossoms of the May,
    Thy snowy spotless white
    And fresh green leaves appear.

The primrose and the violet bloom, in woods
Among their kind; but thou on the bare breast
    Of earth, a single grace,
    When all beside is reft.

Young Flora's messenger before her sent
To herald in her sweet approach; thou com'st
    A token and a pledge,
    A lowly, meek evangel.

To the Snowdrop.

I gaze on thee, and dream the ecstacy
Of spring, the beauty of the spring, whose heart
>	Of mystery shall ope
>	In buds and blooms and glories.

Thou art to me, sweet flower, a thing of joy,
To me thou art a prophecy of beauty,
>	For ever beautiful,
>	For evermore a joy.

A snowdrop amid winter's snow, I too
Would bloom like thee in spotless purity:
>	Like thee would prophesy
>	Of sweetness yet to come.

The Fairy.

Know you a fairy,
Tender and simple,
Smiling and sleek,
Hid in a dimple,
Lodged in a lady's cheek?
Spirit so airy
She hides her and sleeps
Till wildly she leaps,
Flashing out on the sight
Like a sunbeam of light;
Gleaming so brightly,
Tripping all lightly,
Daintiest mirth,
Loveliest birth
That ever was seen,
This fairy I ween.

Sometimes she creeps
Soft from her hiding place,
Winsome in grace,
Tender as bird,

When not a leaf stirred,
Silent she keeps
Watch o'er her nest
Holy and deep.

Soul inly beautiful,
Heart inly dutiful,
Only could keep,
Beautiful spirit of light,
Fairy so gracious and bright,
Softly at rest,
Hid in the dimple,
Tender and simple,
Sweet place of delight.

Titania.

Within an antique wood, where knotty trees
Did over head their branches interweave;
Upon a mossy bank, with flowers bedecked,
Where in the golden noon, the Zephyr soft
Might often rest and cloy his wings with sweets,
Now silvered o'er with the pure moonlight's sheen,
From off that bed of fragrant flowers, methought
I saw upraised a lovely female form:
A pale and lustrous splendour, like the lone star
On evening's brow! dimly in that dim place
Beneath the leafy canopy, it rose—
Titania, queen of fairies in her bower!
A regal grace, with ærial beauty mixed,
Sat on her form: a sweet and dainty charm!
The gossamer and flowing robe did scarce
Her fairy limbs conceal, but through its folds

Their brightness shone, like the pale moon, through veil
Of silvery clouds!   The lotus flower of Ind
Adorned her hair, and at her feet reposed
A sleeping child—a lovely Indian boy!
Sweet music issued from her lips, and filled
The forest glades, and at the sound crept forth
From out a thousand flowers, where all day long
They couched unseen, fairies and fays, and elves:
They came in troops about her feet: with songs
And dance they circled round her flowery bed,
And singing, offered homage to their queen,
Throned in her moonlit bowers!

Timon's Grave.

A SOLITARY grave beside the sea,
Where the green grass grows not, nor herb, nor flower,
Nor tree is near; for on that barren ground
The salt tears of the briny sea fall thick,
And drench with heavy rain the flowerless sod!
Meet resting place for that great broken heart
Which loved too well, and loathed too deep its kind!

The sea-bird floats above the sounding wave.
The mighty wind goes rushing by; their watch
Above the grave the silent stars of heaven
Maintain; but sign or sound of human presence
Desecrate not the awful loneliness!
Nature, in savage, grandest mood is there,
And with bare breast uprises, sombre and wild

And great.   Upon the borders of the flood
Behold the stern Athenian's lonely grave!
Does not that great grand ruin of a man
Find in that place befitting sepulchre?
Those stern and savage attributes around,
Are they not kindred to his spirit as
It passed, estranged, alone, apart from men?

Eternal tears fall on the lowly grave—
What need of human grief?   He asked it
    not.

Fidele.

Oh! silent image, white and still—
Sweet lily, smitten in thy prime!
Can this, indeed, indeed be death
So hush'd, so rapt, so beautiful?
The meek hands folded o'er the breast,
The gentle lips but slightly parted,
As if the breath still crept between:
The white and azured lids that droop
In semblance of a tender sleep:
The rippling waves of golden hair,
The lovely form composed and still,
And o'er each feature softly shed
A beauty of repose ineffable,
As if in dreams some thought of bliss
The raptured spirit dimly held!
Enamoured Death hangs o'er his bride,
And on the tintless marble lips
Doth set his first cold kiss!

                          The last
Red rays of the descending sun
Stream through the open cave, and make
A glory on the sleeper's face

Like halo round a saintly brow.
Silent and mute, with naked feet
The mourners stand beside the dead,
And scarcely with a breath disturb
The awful silence brooding there.
A moment thus they stand, and then
With wailing voice together sing
The mournful requiem of the dead.
The tearful drops of holy sound
Fall on the soft and trancèd air
Sweet as the droppings of the night
That on the heart of the white rose
Distil.

    "No more," they sang, "no more
Shall winter's wind thy rest disturb;
    Nor frownings of the great,
    Nor scornings of the proud—
For thee the home, the rest, remain!
We'll lay thee with thy face toward the east,
Where from the chambers of the dawn
The monarch of the day comes forth,
    That thy first sight
In the bright resurrection morn
May be the glorious sun uprisen
    Upon a smiling world!

With fairest flowers thy grave we'll strew,
Pure as thy purity—sweet as thy youth!"

Kneeling apart, the mournful chant
They raise, with low and broken voice,
Like wailings of the parent bird
That flits above her ravished nest;—
So, till the song in weeping ends,
And the wild music dies in tears!

Ariel.

ARIEL! sweet Ariel
Lovely, tender Ariel!
Come and fold your fairy wings,
Nestle in my thought awhile.
Bird of love, come hither, come!
Come from beds of yellow sand,
Come from ocean's stilly caves,
Where the pearls and coral grow,
Where the sea-maids weave their hair;
Or, if there thou dalliest,
Fairy spirit, at thy play,
Come from 'neath white boughs of May!
Where the bee doth honey suck,
Where the butterfly doth play,
From thy bed in cowslip bell
Wake thee, sprite, and come to me.
Come from curled and glittering clouds,
Fairy dear, if thou be there;
Haste thee, sweet, and come to me,
Bring with thee the mountain nymph,
Bring the naiad of the brook,
Naked maid of lotus flower;
Bring the tribes that nightly haunt
Village green and mystic wood;

Ariel.

Bring the fairy song and dance;
Bring the moonbeams' magic play;
Bring the swell of ocean's wave;
Bring the breath of mountain breeze.
Ring my soul with all thy charms,
Fairy bright, thy witchery sway.

* * * * *

It rises from the poet's page,
Wearing upon its baby brow
A spirit's kingly glory.
A child, with all a young child's taste,
Its love, its sportiveness, its joy—
Yet mighty with a spirit's power
To flash through realms of earth and air;
To tread the salt ooze of the deep,
To pierce the hidden veins of earth,
To read the secret human soul.
Not as bright Oberon; not as
Titania and her fairy train;
Not as the fays that haunt the flowers;
Not as the genii of old tale:
It hath an order of its own.
Of spirit things it stands alone;
Of fairy things it stands apart.
It is an infant glorified,
A child exalted and endowed
With spirit power, yet still a child!

Ophelia.

FAIREST creation of his genius who has
Enriched the mind with noble images,
And shewn us Nature's loveliness unfolded
In the heart of woman, as no man else.
Purest creation of the master's art,
Coldly-pure as the cold ice of her own clime,
Passionless purity no breath has breathed
Upon—the virgin daughter of the north—
The meek Ophelia!

      Love's roseate flush,
If it indeed be love, that tender glow
Which round her plays, falls on her gentle
  youth
As morning's crimson on the stainless lily,
Yet leaves its whiteness still the same: so
  calm,
So virgin-pure her soul, she scarcely knows
She loves, yet dies she of a broken heart.
Not as the lofty, queenly Isabel,
Not as the dark-eyed daughter of the south
Whose being is fire and music; not as

Ophelia.

The lovely Imogen—she stands alone,
Marked with a beauty all her own—the lily
Of the poet's thoughts: there is none like to her.
Methinks, if Nature should a priestess seek
To minister in her inner sanctuary—
A fair and vestal daughter—whose essence should
Be all-unmixed with earthly elements,
This should be she—all-meetest to be such.
But she, alas! is mortal, for she dies:
A woman in her grief and feebleness,
But more than mortal in her purity.
Her mind is a still summer's lake, where all
Sweet shadows gently sleep; the scattered leaf
Upon its bosom motionless reposes.
The night came down upon the waveless waters
Moonless and starless, but no breath of storm
Ruffled its calmness: even in utter madness
Her heart reveals itself unsullied—sweet
And sorrowful her melancholy pours
Its plaint; for from that nature unpollute,
Nothing but purity could ever come,

Nothing but sweetness flow; even from her
 dust
Must violets grow!

                  How faint, how delicate
The lines which trace that northern loveli-
 ness!
How soft its neutral tints! within her heart
Strong filial love burns with a holy flame,
Through which the sorrow-clouds of madness
 shines
Brilliant and clear; but other passion find
You none: there may be such, but if there be,
It rests all-secret in her virgin breast,
And unrevealed remains, for ever veiled.

Her tenderness, her beauty, and her woe
Touch the deep springs of pity in my mind,
The hidden springs of tender memory;
And when I see the willow bends its boughs
Above the glassy stream, I think of her
Who died, as the wild swan dies, in song;
 and
To the sad, sweet tragedy, accord my tears.

Miranda.

MIRANDA, Nature's child, nursed at her breast
So long, thou needs must wear her likeness, and be
In thy simplicity without a guile,
Thou lovely, artless one!

                      The poet's wand
From out the deep that bright enchanted isle
Has raised, with all its fair and shadowy forms,
And fitted to those shapes of loveliness
The solitary maid, so fair, so young,
So delicate! A coy and simple maiden
In budding youth she rises on our sight;
The daughter of that lonely man, whose realms
And empire were the powers invisible;
Who rendered tributary to his will
The airy spirits, and the elves that haunt
The forest caves, or hide in flowery beds.

A gentle, unaffected girl, and yet
The issue of a prince, and held so long
In intercourse with that majestic mind,
She has received a somewhat of its grandeur,
And wears upon her guileless brow imprint
A kindred sovereignty. Over her slumbers
Have Ariel's wings been waved with songs
  of love ;
And the bright spirit's melodies have
  mingled with
Her thoughts till they have caught their
  wildness : wild
And free as the free mountain wind is she—
The maid who never yet has seen the face
Of woman! Yet with a heart open as day
To melting charity ; an eye that weeps
The tears of tenderest pity.—The child
Who cheered with smiles the exile's bitter
  toil ;
The tender pleader for the wrecked ; a thing
Of innocence and joy, with gentlest heart
Attuned to sympathy.

                          Sweet, dainty maid,
We would not have thee other than thou
  art,
The wild flower of the lonely isle, one trait

The more, one touch the less, one beauty
    gone,
Had spoiled the lovely charm; more sweet
    than art,
Great Nature's hand has formed her favourite
    child.

The Well of Samaria.

In Sychar's valley, where on either side
The mounts of Ebal and Gerizim tower,
Deep in the lovely glade, there is a well
Within whose caverned depths, crystal and
    cold,
The delicate waters spring; a fountain formed
In olden time by Abraham's son, even him
Who from the wilds of Syria brought again
His family and flocks: all coldly-pure,
As when at first the patriarch scooped the
    well,
From mighty heighted-hills perennial fed,
Gush th' unfailing waters, and afford
Blessing and ever fresh delight.

                                The noon
With burning radiance floods the mount and
    plain,
From the high mountain peaks, to the soft
    line
Of nearer hills, and the fair valley's slopes

Mellowed to tenderer beauty, all the scene
Is bathed in living light; cloudlessly pure,
Of brightest sapphire, through its vast expanse,
Suffused with golden fire, the lofty heaven
Appears. It is the hour of highest noon:
The sycamore, whose branches lately cast
Fantastic shadows on the ground, now throws
No shade; the gardens where the citron and
The olive grow, where the pomegranate blooms,
And where the creeping vine trails on the ground
Her boughs, are shadowless; on trellised slopes
And fertile plains, the noon-tide glory burns—
So clear, so brilliant, and yet pure and soft,
That glowing atmosphere! On the wooded hills
Afar the golden light dissolves itself
To amethyst, and softly wraps them round
With violet vapours.

      Gigantic trees beside
The patriarch's well, weave with tenebrous boughs
A grateful shade, beneath the sultry noon,

Sweet as the rest the chosen people found
Beneath the palms by Elim's springs of old.
The clambering vine beside the well sends o'er
Its walls her boughs, and interlaced with many
A climbing plant and fragrant shrub, with flowers
Of glorious hue inwrought, a covert forms
Of thickest leaves, through which the sunlight falls
With tempered ray. Beneath that shadowy arch
Of pendent leaves a stranger sits,—alone,
And weary; on his garments and his feet
The dust of travel lies; mean is his garb,
But on his face grandeur and majesty
Soften to tenderness ineffable,
And speak the lofty soul.

      It is the Christ,
Even He whom kings and seers in days long past
In strains of dim prophetic lore foretold,
Whose dayspring from afar Abraham hailed
Rejoicing; to whose dawn the purer minds
Of earth expectant turned; Supreme Desire

Of nations, after whom the world's great
 heart,
With dumb instinctive longing yearned, yea,
 even
In heathen lands and darkest times: the
 crown
And the completeness of humanity,
The flower of the human race! Oh, won-
 drous Man!
Oh, glorious birth of woman! Heavenly Son
Of Mary!

        The unique and wondrous beauty,
Whose infancy the lowly Nazareth nursed,
Has come to ripe perfection; the green corn
Matured and mellowed all its ears: even
 now
On human eyes hath beamed that wondrous
 grace;
Even now doth all the fulness of its glory
Abide with men, and yet they know it not!
Veiling Himself beneath a servant's form,
He meekly suffers contumely and shame,
Refused and scorned, He only renders
 blessing,
And unto these His enemies extends
His hands in love!

                    And 'thus in lowliest guise
Behold, He sits beside Samaria's well,
Hither from Judah journeying on His way
Toward Galilee of the Gentiles: yea, see
In weariness He there reposes Him,
Although Divine, yet touched with human
        weakness,
Thou lowly, lowly Christ!

                        Pure in their fount
The waters spring, but purer in His heart
The deep sweet love, the inexhaustible
Waters of a divine beneficence.
With Him abides the fount of life, the source
From whence the streams and tributary
        rivers
Through all creation flow with life and heal;
Hither as to their spring, the heavenly
        powers
And hierarchies repairing draw their glory,
And thence all lovely things derive their
        beauty!

There solitary by the well He sits,
Weary, alone,—for of that faithful band
Of Israel's nobler sons who walk with Him,
The few who now accompany their Lord

The Well of Samaria.

On needful errand sent, lately went hence.
He is alone in the deep solitude:
No sound of human voice falls on the ear,
Nor footstep there: (angels invisible
Afar on resting wing wait silently,
Nor rush unbidden on His presence,) so hushed,
So quiet the scene! sweet and gentle sounds
Float on the air; there is an influence,
A charm of sweetness inexplicable
In that soft hour and place, as if it came
In recognition dimly of His glory,
Who sits amid those beauteous works, whereof
He is Creator; the awed and silent earth
Doth feel the touch of those immaculate feet,
And with a dim faint movement feebly greets
Her Kingly Guest; not so the garden smiled,
When through its glorious paths its Maker's steps
Echoed, and Paradise resplendent glowed
More beautiful!

   Come with thine offspring, earth;

Come with thy birds and flowers and living
    things;
Come with thy noblest growths, great
    mother, come!
And to thy lowly King thine offerings bring
From out thy realms.

     The hushed waves of the sea
Adored Him, and with soft murmurs kissed
    His feet,
When at His word the stormy wind assuaged
Its rage, and sank to deepest calm; even so
In days of trial in the wilderness,
The beasts of prey their fierceness quelled,
    and grew
Submissive at His presence.

       O'er the scene
A solemn beauty dawns, and like the bliss
Of an ecstatic dream its sweetness sheds,
For there are moments when in awe, to Him
The powers of nature homage yield, and
    those
Sublimities which sleep within her breast,
Awake to give Him praise: and such are
    now.
The lordly eagle darting in his flight

Toward his rock-built nest, hangs in the air
Entranced, and the white dove on quiet wing
Steals to his breast; from 'mong the olive groves
The turtle's voice is heard with softer note,
And round His feet the young fair flowers that grow,
More sweet their virgin bloom and grateful scent
For Him distil: such in her bridal wreath
The first of women wore, with drops of dew
Impearled, pure as her heart, which knew no guile.

What are His thoughts in that still lonely hour,
Who shall conceive or speak? what hand unveil
The mystery of that purity? how lift
The covering of its sacredness? not untouched
Of outward things, but swaying with each motion,
Changing,—yet perfect equally in all,—
How moves that gentle scene, a mind wherein
Each tender influence its beauty weaves?
For unto Him the future and the past

Are as an open book, yet in His heart
In measure due the present hath a place,
And every delicate relationship,
So exquisitely pure its perfect part.
It may be that His glance pierces the gloom
Of ages past, the dim abysm of time,
Before, in this our lower universe
Creation travailed in birth, or life was formed;
Or with an all-pervading vision sweeps
Futurity, and where the mighty times
Converge, rests on that fair perfection of
Creation reared to the sublimest heights
Of its great Author's thoughts, when in the kingdom
Of the Father each form of life shall come
To full and beautiful development,
And Nature all her goodly fruits mature,
Untouched of evil through th' unbounded realms!
Perchance His thoughts hang o'er a lonely bier,
A bier whereon erewhile a maiden lay,
A white and unpolluted lily, in
The beauty of her youth smote down by death.
See through the marble lips the new warm breath·

The Well of Samaria.

Respires, she lives, she breathes, she speaks
    His name
Not to her heart unknown: or it may be
He lovingly remembers the young child
He lately held in His embrace! on whom
He laid His hands in blessing! vain search—
    enough
That He is weary, and those blessèd feet,
Which moved but to do good, are worn with
    toil.
No further may we lift the veil; enough
To trace with reverent thought His weari-
    ness,
Who from the highest heaven humbled
    Himself
Thus low!

        A footstep on the silence falls,
A solitary step,—a woman steals
On the reposing Christ; with hand upraised
Her water-vessel on her head she bears.
Hither she comes, the daughter of Samaria,
To draw from out the well where oft resort
The women of the city. She moves into
The immediate presence of the glorious
    One,
Yet ignorant, unconscious, she not thinks,

Nor dreams, that underneath that lowly form
The Majesty of Israel hides. She stands
Before Him face to face, conceiving not
The glory veiled: but who is she who thus
Approaches the All-pure? Is she as those
Who pure in heart behold the face of God
Mirrored as on deep waters,—His image bright
Refulgent shining in their own soul's depths?
Alas! the white and unstained snow no more
Is white: the garments of her womanhood
Are stained with the foul spots of sin; the flower
The spotless virgin rose—has dropped its leaves
To foul decay. Upon her countenance
There is a strange and troubled look, the shade
Of inward darkness, the deep gloom of soul.
She has been beautiful; but grief, or crime,
Or both, have marred the beauty of her face;
And o'er the lineaments, which once were fair,
Destroying fingers swept. He looks on her
With gaze in which a deep compassion yearns,

The pity of divinest love! He traces
In her life's sad past, the first step astray;
The wrong, and the temptation, the deep fall
And bitter consequence therefrom evolved;
The deep dark sin, the misery, the shame,
Speak but to wake His pity, and call forth
A more exceeding grace, mercy more large!
Shall He not rescue, and o'ercome with good,
Who came to save the lost. and utterly
Destroy the works of evil? Through His voice,—
His eye,—trembles the utterance of a love,
Which wins its way to her most secret soul.
A dim sweet thrill, a new and spiritual sense
Is rising in her heart; she has perceived
A light, a purity, a tenderness
Before unknown; the halo of a great light
Seen from afar through clouds and mist, which but
For all her guilt, her sin, had been more clear.
And with it comes a troubled memory
Of the past, a longing, wistful backward glance:
She sees with misty eyes a happy home
In a green vale, where mountain waters fall
And glide, and in its light two figures move,

A gentle mother and a young fair girl,
A virgin in the dawn of womanhood:
She sees not that which is around, nor Him
Who speaks with her, but o'er her misty
    eyes
That flickering vision floats; and on her ear
A sound of falling waters heard afar,
Comes as the refrain of a dying song.
Far, far away, the blissful vision swims!
Sweet saddening memory of that happy
    time
Wherein a stainless purity was hers,
Mournful remembrancer what now she is.
The large tears drop, they fall, they bathe
    His feet,
She bows her at the feet of Christ and
    weeps!
With gentleness as beautiful as that
The shepherd shows when in the wilderness
He finds the wandering sheep, and tenderly
Upon his shoulders lays the wearied one,
He deals with her; in His most perfect love
Touching with reverent hand the poor sore
    heart.
He speaks of Him who bears a Father's
    name,
The great All-Father, whose paternal heart

Enfolds alike all races as His offspring,
The Spirit, Infinite, invisible,
Whose essence unconfined is everywhere
Adored; viewless and inconceivable,
Yet ever near, and filling with Himself
The outstretched human arms; the great
   first source,
Who in Himself contains, concentres all,
The Father universal, who must be
Even as a Spirit in spirit and in truth
Adored.

   Slowly the vast conception breaks
Upon her mind: as its stupendous parts
Unroll, the thought of the great Father,
   with
An all-embracing love, enwraps her heart.
Lowly she kneels before the Saviour's feet,
While from the hidden glory in Himself
He lifts the veil of seeming lowliness,
The Christ by His own lips to her declared.
She sees in Him,—with soul adoring sees,—
The face of God revealed, the beautiful
Reflection of the unseen Infinite,
The image of the Highest! there, alone,
Alone with Christ,—she finds in that deep
   love

Which pardons all her sins, her perfect rest:
All fears, all cares, have passed away, and left
Before her soul a solitary grandeur,
The glorious One who thus with her communes.

Meanwhile, the twelve returned, stand round their Lord,
And mark with wondering looks her business there:
She startles at their presence, and with thanks
And murmured blessing, arises and departs,
Leaving her water-vessels there unfilled.

And much they marvel that He spake with her,
The woman of an alien race, which hath
In Israel's fold no place; yet in His eye,
And on His countenance there is a look,
Forbids the question trembling on their lips,
" Master, why talkest Thou with her?" They yield—
Silently yield submission to His will,
Yet comprehend Him not. Oft have they seen

His gracious deeds in varied scene and place,
The hungry fed, the sick, the leper touched
And healed, and in that pure beneficence
Which grew beneath their gaze, admiringly
Have traced the beauty of that mind, which wrought
The delicate lily's grace: but now, alas!
They understand Him not; they know not yet
That grace divine the Saviour came to show,
How God in infinite embrace should gather
The families of men, and give to them,
Who were by former dispensation banned,
A place as children near. Imperfectly
Have they received the message of that love
The heavenly Teacher taught, and poorly learned
The greatness of His mighty heart.

          He sees
Prophetic, the future harvest of the earth,
The promised great ingathering, and bids them look
On whitening fields; no grain shall perish, nor
One field be left unreaped, nor cluster left

To fall ungleaned, when the great Lord of harvest
Shall gather in His Pentecostal fruits.
Blessèd is he who reaps, and blessèd he
Who goeth forth bearing the precious seed,
For both shall joy together in that day.

He has attuned their hearts to harmony
With His, touched with a kindred thought: they stand
Silent and hushed, and of His spirit take.

But who are these who break upon the view?
Down the green paths that slope from yonder town,
Through sunny paths that 'mong the vineyards wind,
Through groves with fragrant myrtles lined, they pour,
They rush, a gathering crowd. She comes again
Who lately proved the Saviour's grace and truth,—
Nor she alone—but lo! Samaria pours
Its people forth: trooping they hither come,
Attracted by her words, which told of Him

The more than prophet, the long-promised
    Christ
At length revealed; the mighty One, whose
    fame
Has reached them as a sound from Galilee,
Where first in act of miracle He put
His glory forth, blessing with gracious gift
The feast in Cana's halls. Onward they
    flow,
Intent the Christ to find: He lifts His eyes,
And from afar beholds th' approaching
    throng,
And moving forward, meets with outstretched
    hands
The first of the advancing host. But see,
They come, they throng, they press around
    the Lord,
All breathless on His robes they hang, while
    He
Responsive meets them with His wonted
    grace,
And to them speaks the words of truth:
    entranced
They cluster round and gladly list His word.
The mother with her babe is there; the hoar
And aged man leans listening on his staff,
And softly to His side the young child steals,

While from His lips there falls the melting tale
Of heavenly love, the sweetest parable
Of all, the story of the Father's love
In earthly image shown, the lost one found.
For many a time and oft did those sweet lips
Repeat the never-tiring tale. More close
They draw, while drop on each attentive ear
The tender words of the great parable.
And many a weeping eye may there be seen,
And many a form of woman gently bowed,
While o'er the crowd some wild grand head upreared,
With eyes of earnest gaze, tells that some mind
Of loftier mould the Master's wisdom owns.
Anon with eagle flight He carries them
Beyond the bounds of sight, then droops and sweeps
With lower scope the range of earthly things.
With touches of a woman's tenderness,
He brightens into life some simple scene,
A group of waving lilies in the field,
A shepherd watching o'er the fold—and wakes
In every heart some chord of sympathy.

With noble imagery built grandly up
He shadows on their souls the Infinite,
And wakes in them the mystic spirit-sense,
The human yearning after God. He calls,
He leads them up to heights before unknown
Of moral purity, and there unfolds
The law of a diviner charity!
He passes not beyond the heart of each,
And yet it is a new morality,
The purest ethics, the sublimest truths
In simplest form declared, from the deep heart
Of all things drawn. From the pure breast of Nature
He has evoked His laws, and they shall stand
Immutable, Heaven's highest will.

         All swift
The time flies by,—swiftly the hours have sped;
The mellowed beauty of the sunset falls
Around that sacred form, and o'er the crowd
That throng around, its softened splendours stream.
Each lowly object has the radiance caught,
Flushing with tints all lovely, the reflex

Of that sea of gold that rolls its glory-tide
Afar, into the deep infinity!
Each tree, each bush, each small and trembling leaf,
Stands glorified in the warm living light.
At such an hour the heavens draw near the earth,
And earth becomes transformed, until it seems
Itself so beautiful of them a part!
Even so the glory of that heavenly One
There in the people's midst pours over them
Its light ineffable, its tender glow!
Awhile the beauty of the highest heaven
Has opened over men, and on them sheds
Its sweet and wondrous glory, till each heart,
Each tender human feeling, wakes responsive,
And e'en the dulled affections of the darkened soul
Grow beautiful with its mysterious touch.

Oh! living Light, the prime and increate,
In which there is no darkness; heavenly Sun,
Shine on our souls, and over all pour forth
Thy rays; yea, to that dim eternity
Upon whose shore the unknown ages break,
Pour Thy full tides of glory, till all life

Glow in Thy life, and Thou in it, and it
In Thee be glorified! Rise Thou on us,
And permeate our lives, our thoughts, our deeds,
Making them with Thy beauty beautiful!

Swiftly the hours glide by, while on His words
They hang: the sun has sunk beneath the hills,
The young pale moon arises in the sky,
The moon and trembling evening star,—while melts
By finest graduations into night
The glowing day. Silence falls on the people—
A momentary hush, to break anon
In rapturous words; "Master and Lord," they pray,
"Saviour and Lord, abide with us! depart
Not Thou, forsake us not! Our eyes have seen,
Our ears have heard the Saviour of the world!
Rise fairest Star, Sceptre of Jacob, rise,
And o'er our hearts Thy sweetest influence sway.

The Seraphim attendant on His glory,
Which from the highest rank of heavenly
    powers
Were called obedient to His will, even they,
Who in creation's dawn when o'er the face
Of chàos the Creator moved, with wings
Of burning light enclosed Him round, and
    woke
The void of silence with triumphal chants;
Even as the flame all swift their ministry
And pure their essence,—these His ministers,
Attendant on His earthly mission, watch
With raptured gaze that scene of wondrous
    grace;
Partaking in His joy, exultingly
They raise their joys, high above thought
    or words,
Seraphic gladness!

                        Samaria's well,
Where erst the Saviour sat, I linger there
With unshod feet; and sacred to my soul
Becomes the place where Jesus humbled
    thus
His glory, and stooping thus, the lowly
    raised!

LIST OF SUBSCRIBERS.

Abrahall Rev. T. H., M.A., Butterleigh (2 copies)
Abbott Mr., Bideford
Ackland Dr., ditto
Allen Rev. W., ditto
Albrecht C., Esq., Exeter (2)
A Friend, Exeter
Adams Mr., Senr., Torrington
Adams Mr. R., ditto (2)
Adams Mr. J., ditto
A Gentleman, ditto (2)
A Friend, ditto
A Friend, ditto
Ashton Mrs., ditto
Ashton Mrs. W., Burwood, ditto
Ashplant Mr., ditto
Allen Mrs., Barnstaple
Adams Mrs., ditto
Ashton R., Esq., ditto
Alford Mrs., Braunton
Adams J., Esq., Greenwich
A Friend, Plymouth
Alford Mr., Wear Gifford
Abbott Mr., Frithelstock
Arnold G., Esq., Dolton
Arnold W., Esq., ditto
Arnold Miss, Beaford
Ashton Miss, Merton
Barnes Revd. R. H., M.A., Heavitree
Beer Miss, Torrington (2)
Brierly Rev. J., B.A., ditto (2)
Bangham Mr., ditto
Bangham Mrs. T., ditto
Bastard Mr., ditto
Brown Miss, ditto
Blake Mr., ditto
Buckland Mrs., Vicarage, ditto
Bazeley Rev. F., M.A., Rector of Bideford
Bazeley —, Esq., ditto
Bate Mrs. E., ditto
Baker Mr. T., ditto
Babbage Mrs., ditto
Bale Mr, ditto
Barrow Mrs., ditto
Braund Mrs., ditto
B. A., ditto
Bishop Mr., ditto
Burroughs Mr., ditto
Benson —, Esq., Appledore
Beard Mr. J., ditto
Brooks Mrs., ditto
Budd Dr., Barnstaple
Barry Mr J., ditto
Bowden Mrs., ditto
Bencraft T., Esq., ditto
Bencraft L., Esq., ditto
Bertram Rev. R., ditto
Baker Mr, ditto
Brown G., Esq., ditto (2)
Beardsworth Mr. G. E., London
Bridgewater Mr. E., ditto
Burridge Mrs., ditto
Brinsmead Mr., ditto
Burrington Mr., Exeter
Bluett Miss, Mt. Radford, ditto
Barr Dr., Aldershot (2)
Browne Mrs., Trowbridge
Bethune Mrs, Chumleigh
Balsdon Mr., Southcott
Balsdon Mr., Wear Gifford
Bishop Mr., Roborough
Badcock Mr., ditto
Bennett Miss, ditto
Bradford Mr., St. Giles

List of Subscribers.

Brinsmead Mr., St. Giles
Balsdon Mr., ditto
Bartlett Mrs., Frithelstock
Brine Revd. G. A., M.A., Frithelstock
Bickham Mrs., Merton
Barker Mrs, Ilkley (2)
Barker Mrs. W., ditto
Butcher H., Esq., High Bickington
Browne Rev. B., Barnstaple
Badcock Mr., Torpoint
Coleridge Sir John, Attorney General (2)
Chapple N., Esq., Mayor of Torrington
Chapple Miss, ditto
Clarke Mr., ditto
Copp Miss S., ditto
Copp Mr. J., ditto
Copp Mrs., Moretown
Carter Mrs., ditto
Chanter T. B., Esq., Bideford
Cox Mr, ditto
Capel Hon. Capt., Woodtown House, Bideford
Channel Mrs., ditto
Cox —, Esq., ditto
Croscombe Mrs., ditto
Crang Miss, ditto
Cox Mr. R., Appledore
Churchard Revd. M. D. D., Northam
Cook M., Esq., Barnstaple
Chanter T. R., Esq., Fort Hill, Barnstaple
Chichester Sir Bruce, Arlington, Barnstaple
Crasswaller C., Esq., Mayor of Barnstaple
Currie —, Esq., ditto
Cockram Miss, ditto
Cooper Mr., London (2)
Cook J., Esq., ditto
Colby Rev. F., Exeter
Coldridge Mrs., ditto
Cummings W. R., Esq., ditto

Chamberlain Miss, Heavitree (2)
Copp Miss, Kingscot
Capern E., Esq., Birmingham
Channel Mr, Richmond
Chevalier J., Esq., Manchester (2)
Chevalier E. J., Esq., Liverpool (2)
Coham W. B., Esq., Highampton
Cann Mr., Plymouth
Cooper G., Esq., Wear Gifford
Chammings Mrs., ditto
Cato Mr., Merton
Clements Mrs., Roborough
Croscombe Mr., ditto
Clarke Mr., St. Giles
Causey Mrs., Little Torrington
Chambers Mr., Dolton
Clinton The Right Hon. Lord, Heanton Satchville (3)
Cooper Miss, Monkleigh
Copp Mrs., Langtree
Copp Mrs J., ditto
Cawker J, Esq., Swansea
Cawker Mrs. R. J., ditto (2)
Cawker Miss, ditto
Cocks Mr., Torquay
Cann G., Esq., South Tawton
Cann Mr., ditto
Cole Mr. F., Bideford
Cave T., Esq., M.P., East Sheens
Chichester Mrs., Rectory, Clovelly
Chichester Sir Arthur, Youlston
Devon Right Hon. The Earl of
Doe G., Esq., Torrington
Doe Miss, ditto (2)
Doe Mrs. C., ditto
Doidge S., Esq., ditto
Down Mr., Bideford
Down Miss, ditto
Dingle Mr., ditto
Douell Mrs., Ford, ditto
Daymond Mrs., Northam Road
Dunn Miss, ditto

List of Subscribers.

Darracott Captain, Appledore
Dendle Mr., Barnstaple
Dart Mr., Exeter
Deane W. A., Esq., Webbery
Drew Mrs., Grange Honiton
Downing Mr., Wear Gifford
Dart Mrs., ditto
Drawer Mr., St. Giles
Down Mr., Cardiff (6)
Drew H., Esq., Exeter
Dawson J. W., Esq , London
Down Miss, Torpoint
Down Mr., Darlington
Down Miss, Newport
Drawer Mr., Little Torrington
Eastmond Mr., Torrington
Endicott Mr., Little Silver, ditto
Embrey Mr., Bideford
Evans T., Esq., Northam Road
Eddiford T., Esq., London
Edmunds Mr., ditto
Ellis Mrs. K., Exeter
Evans Mr., Dolton
Edwards Rev. E., Torquay
Fairchild Mr., Torrington
Fisher G., Esq., ditto
Farleigh Mr , ditto
Fowler Mr., ditto
Fowler Miss, ditto
Friendship Mrs., Sen., ditto
Friendship Miss, ditto
Furse Miss, Bideford
Ford Miss, Northam Ridge
Forester Dr., Barnstaple
Ffinch J. P., Esq., ditto
Farleigh R., Esq., ditto
Farrington Revd. E. H., B.A., Landcross
Fowler Revd. H., Gloucester (2)
Ferris Mrs., Plymouth (2)
Fisher Miss, Frithelstock
Furse Rev. C. W., Staines
Fisher A. B., Esq., Butterleigh
Fowler C., Esq., Torquay
Freeman Mrs., Coombe Torrington

Fletcher J., Esq., Warren House, Torrington
Gawtrey Miss, Torrington
Glubb P B., Esq., ditto
Gratton Miss, ditto
Guard Mr., ditto
Garland Mr., ditto
Gunn Mr., ditto
Gibson Dr. Burns, ditto
Goaman Mr., ditto
Good Mr., ditto
Geoghegan Mr. J , ditto
Gum Col., Northam Road
Gossett Rev. T. H., Westward Ho
Gamble C. H., Esq., Barnstaple
Gould W., Esq , ditto
Gould R. D., Esq., ditto
Gammon Mr., ditto
Guppy T., Esq., ditto
Greenslade Miss, Minehead
Gaydon Mr., Kingston on Thames
Gurney Rev. W., LL.B., Roborough
Guille Rev. G. De, M.A., Little Torrington
Guille Mrs., ditto
Goss Mr., Merton
Guard Rev. J., M.A., Langtree
Godfrey Miss, Torquay
Guest Mrs., Bristol
Hole C., Esq., Torrington
Hole Miss, ditto
Hole Miss A., ditto
Hole A., Esq., Beam House, Torrington
Handford Mr., ditto
Holwill Mrs., ditto
Holwill Miss, ditto
Hoyten Mr., ditto
Heywood Mr., ditto
Hooper Mr., ditto
Hole C., Esq., Bideford
How J., Esq., Mayor of ditto (2)
Heard Miss, ditto
Heywood Mr., ditto

List of Subscribers.

Hodges Mr., Bideford
Hooper Mrs., ditto
Hogg Mr., ditto
Hatherly W. F. W., Esq., ditto
Hill Mr., ditto
Hookway Mr , ditto
Hunshi Col., Northam Road
Hutchinson General, ditto
Harper J., Esq., Barnstaple
How A., Esq., ditto
Hortop H., Esq , ditto
Hookway Miss S., Fremington
Havel Mrs., Willows, London (2)
Heath Mr. J. P., Southerny, Exeter
Hodges Mr., ditto
Heath Miss A. B., Heavitree
Hooper Mrs., Keanton
Herniman Mrs., Bradiford
Heywood Mr., Winkleigh
Hutton Captain, Glen Cottage
Hoyten Miss, Plymouth
Hoyten Mr. J. R., Torpoint
Heywood Mrs., Stonehouse
Hackett Miss, Wear Gifford
Harris Mr , ditto
Harris Miss, Roborough
Hookway Mrs., Sen., ditto
Hookway Mrs., Jun., ditto
Huskins Mr., St. Giles
How Mr., Little Torrington
Hayman Mr. G., Dolton
Hearn J., Esq., Beaford
Hooper Mrs., Marland
Hole Mrs., Bishopsteignton
Holland Miss, Torquay
Hackwell Mr., Langtree
Holwill Miss, Exeter
Hiern J. G., Esq., Castle House, Barnstaple
Jackson Mr. J., Jun., Torrington
Jackson T., Esq., ditto
Jones Dr., ditto
Johnson Miss, Moor House, Torrington (2)
Jenkins Rev. T., Bideford
Joce Mr., Bideford
Joce Mr., Barnstaple
Jackson Rev. T., Launceston
Julian Miss, Cornwall
Jones H., Esq., Wear Gifford
Johnson Mrs., Cross House, Little Torrington
Johnson Miss, Staines (2)
Jeffries Mr., Bristol
Kingdon J. B., Esq., Torrington
Kingdon Miss, ditto
Kingsley Rev. Canon, Eversley
King D , Esq., Bideford
Kitchen Rev. J., Head Master of Grammar School, Bideford
Knill Mr. W., Barnstaple (2)
Kimber Mr. C. W., Exeter
Kidwell Mrs., Wear Gifford
Knapman Miss, Beaford
Kempe Rev. Preb., Merton
Lopes Sir Massey, Maristow, Plymouth
Lee Mr., Torrington
Lockyer Miss E., ditto
Loveband Mrs., ditto
Loftus Mrs., Torrington
Lloyd Mrs., ditto
Lowater Mr., ditto
Long Mrs., ditto
Lee Mr., Bideford
Lee Mr. W., ditto
Long Mr., ditto
List Miss, Northam Road
Leslie Rev. T. G., Appledore
Law Dr., Barnstaple (2)
Law T. H. Esq., ditto
Lake Mr., ditto
Lander A., Esq., ditto
Ling Mrs., Braunton
Lake Mr., London
Latimer T., Esq., Exeter
Larking Mr J., Maidstone
Lockyer B., Esq., Dulverton
Lovell Mrs., Wear Gifford
Lake Mr , ditto
Lake Mr., St. Giles

List of Subscribers.

Lowe Miss, Winscott House, Peters Marland
Liverton Mrs., Beaford
Longney Mr., Swansea
Longney Miss, ditto (2)
Loveband Rev. A. W., Pilton Abbey, Barnstaple
Macartney Mrs., Torrington
Martin Miss, ditto
Medland Mr., ditto
Mallet Mr. J., ditto
Mc Kelvie Mrs., ditto
Moon Mr., ditto
Morfill Mr., ditto
Main Miss, Bideford
Marsh Mr. G., ditto
Monkleigh Mr., ditto
Monkleigh Mr. H., ditto
Morrison R., Esq., Barnstaple
Mc Donald Mr., ditto
May Mr., Jun., ditto
Moon Mrs. G., London (3)
Moore Mr. J. H., Exeter
Mallett Mrs., Frithelstock
Michell S., Esq., Dolton
Mallet Mrs., Swansea
Maxwell T. G., Esq., Okehampton
May T., Esq., Barnstaple
Narraway T., Esq., Bideford
Newcombe Mr., ditto
Norman Mrs., ditto
Norton Locke, Esq., ditto
Nichols Mr. R., ditto
Nichols Mr. W., Appledore
Nicklin Mr., Barnstaple
Narraway W. F., Esq., Blackheath
Norris Mr., St. Giles
Norman Mr., ditto
Norman Mr., Frithelstock
Norman Mrs., Sen., ditto
Norman Miss, ditto
Nichols Miss A., Swansea
Oatway Mr., Bideford
Ongley Mr. W., London
Owen A., Esq., Black Torrington
Palmer Rev. C. E., Torrington
Palmer Col., ditto
Pettle Mr., ditto
Pugh Miss, Moor House, ditto (2)
Pidgeon Mr., ditto
Pearce Mr. S., ditto
Pearce Mr. J., ditto
Penhorwood Mr., ditto
Pedler Mrs., Bideford
Pedler Miss F., ditto
Parsons Mrs., ditto
Parry J. A., Esq., ditto
Pyke Mrs. Ford, ditto
Pyke B., Esq., ditto
Pridham Mr., ditto
Priscott Mr., ditto
Peard G., Esq., ditto
Pollard Mr. G., ditto
Partridge Captain, Northam Rd.
Pratt Dr. C., Appledore
Pickard Mr. W., ditto
Prideaux Mrs., Barnstaple
Peake Mr., ditto
Pigot Rev. J. T., M.A., Fremington
Payne J., Esq., Blackheath
Payne Mrs., ditto
Portsmouth The Countess of
Petherick Mrs., Heavitree
Pim Mrs., ditto
Parson Mrs., Plymouth
Peake Mrs., Stonehouse
Pearce Mrs., Beaford
Plowman Mr., ditto
Passmore Mr., Marland
Passmore Mr. J., ditto
Peard Mr., Monkleigh
Partridge Mrs., ditto
Pitt Mrs. T., Obernforde Butterleigh
Pitt Mrs. G., Lympstone
Pitman Mrs. Emma R., Melbourne Port
Pease Mrs. H. F., Darlington
Pease Mrs. J. Beaumont, ditto (2)
Page Mrs., Roborough

M

List of Subscribers.

Pasmore Mr. W. S., Exeter
Pollard Mr. W., ditto
Pettle Mr., Week, Torrington
Penny R. G., Esq., Bishopsteignton
Reed Rev. W. B., Torrington
Rouse Mrs. R. A., ditto
Rudd Mr., ditto
Rude Mr., ditto
Rooker J., Esq., Bideford
Risdon J., Esq., ditto
Restarick Mr., ditto
Reynolds Rev. E., B.A., Appledore
Rock W. F., Esq., London (7)
Rock Mrs. R., Blackheath
Rock Mrs. H., ditto
Rawlins Mr., Exeter
Rose Miss, ditto (7)
Rouse L., Esq., Sheepwash
Rolle Lady Gertrude, Stevenstone
Risdon W., Esq., Dolton
Risdon Miss, ditto
Ramson J. L., Esq., Bishopsteignton (3)
Ramson Mrs., ditto (3)
Ramson Rev. J. L., Jamaica
Rutter Mr. J. H., Ireland
Rutter Mrs. J. H., ditto
Rouse E., Esq., Bradworthy
Rouse Ezekiel, Esq., M.D., ditto
Russell Rev. J., Dennington (2)
Rolle The Hon. Mark, Stevenstone (2)
Snell Mrs., Torrington
Sing Mr., ditto
Sandford Mr. J. Jun., ditto
Sandford Mr. R., ditto
Sandford Miss C., ditto
Sanford Mr. H., ditto
Slee Mr., ditto
Smith Mr., ditto
Salter Mr., ditto
Spear Rev. J. W., ditto
Stapleton Mr., ditto
Smale Mr., Torrington
Stocker Miss M., ditto
Sellick Mr., Bideford
Smart Miss, ditto
Smale C., Esq., ditto
Squires Mr., ditto
Sinkins Mrs., ditto
Saunders Mr. T. C., ditto
Squires Mr. F., ditto
Swindale Miss S., Appledore
Shapland Miss, Barnstaple
Spooner Mr., ditto
Snell Mr., ditto
Stewart Mr., ditto
Seldon T., Esq., ditto
Stevenson Rev. —, ditto
Skemp Rev. C , Brierly Hill (12)
Symons Mr., Fremington
Sparke Miss S. H., London (2)
Symons R., Esq., ditto (2)
Snodgrass Mr., Exeter
Strong Miss, ditto
Stevens Mrs. Moore, Winscott House, Peters Marland (2)
Stripp Mrs., Plymouth
Sanson Mrs., ditto
Stoneman Mr., ditto
Shapland Mr., Wear Gifford
Sillifant Mrs., Rectory, ditto
Squires Mrs., Roborough
Squires Miss, ditto
Swan Mrs., St. Giles
Squires Mrs., ditto
Sandford Mrs., Frithelstock
Smale Mrs., ditto
Smale Mrs. J., ditto
Scott Captain Smytham, Little Torrington
Squance Mrs., ditto
Snell Mr., Beaford
Snell Mrs., Merton
St. John Mrs., Torquay
Sellick W., Esq., Taunton (2)
Sellick Miss, ditto (2)
Shapland Mr., South Molton
Tapley Mr. J., Torrington
Tanton Mr. E. Hill, ditto

List of Subscribers.

Toms Mr. W., Jun., Torrington
Thompson Dr., Bideford
Tedrake Mr., ditto
Taylor Miss, ditto
Tardrew Mr., ditto
Trewin T., Esq., ditto
Turner G., Esq , ditto
Taylor Lowman, Esq., London (2)
Tupman Miss, ditto
Telfer Rev. E. A., Glasgow
Telfer Miss, Heavitree
Thomas Mr. J. James, Crediton
Thorne T., Esq., Instow
Tucker Mr., Buckland Brewer
Trewaves Mr., Plymouth
Till Mr., St. Giles
Turner Miss F., Beaford
Taylor Mr., Exeter
Thomas Mr. H. D., ditto
Topham Mr., ditto
Trefusis The Honble. Ellen, London
Taylor Mr., Swansea
Thomas A. E., Esq., Court Herbert Neath
Timewell Mr. G. T., Bristol
Tucker Mr. W., Petroikstow
Vallack H. A., Esq., Torrington
Vaughan Mr., ditto
Vaughan Mr. J., ditto
Vaughan Mr. T., ditto
Vincent Mr., ditto
Vodden Mr. Week, ditto
Vodden Mr. L., St. Giles
Vellacott Miss M., Bideford
Vibert Mrs., ditto
Vinson Mr., ditto
Vicary T. M., Esq., Plymouth
Vallence Mrs. A., Melbourne Port
Vallence Miss L., ditto
Webber Mrs., Torrington
Winter Mrs., ditto
Williams Miss, ditto
Williams Miss, Burwood, ditto
Wills Miss, Torrington
Ward Mr., ditto
White Mrs., ditto
Whitemore Mrs., ditto
Warden Miss, ditto (2)
Walkey Mr. G., ditto
Whitaker Mr. G., Bideford
D. R. W., ditto
White E., Esq. (2)
Wilcock Mr., ditto
Walters Mrs., ditto
Withycombe Mr. E. G., ditto
Williams Captain J., Appledore
Ward Mr., Westward Ho
White R., Esq., Customs, Barnstaple
Willshire Mrs., ditto
Worth Mr., London
Williams J. E., Esq., Regent's Park
Widlake P., Esq., Ilfracombe
Wheaton Mrs., Exmouth
Wills C., Esq., Dursley
Woollcombe Rev. L., M.A, Petrockstow
Wadland Mrs., Roborough
Watkins Mr., ditto
Widlake Mr., ditto
Ward Mrs., Little Torrington
Wilson Mrs., ditto
Ward Mrs., ditto
Westland Mrs., Okehampton
Whale Rev. W., M.A., Dolton
Willett Rev. C. S., M.A., Monkleigh
Westcott Miss, Beaford
Wood Rev. C., M.A., ditto
Whitworth Mr. F. J., Birmingham
Yeo Mrs., Richmond House, Appledore
Young Mrs., Torrington
Youings Mr. W., Barnstaple
Youatt Mr., Torpoint

JARROLD AND SONS, PRINTERS, NORWICH.

CPSIA information can be obtained
at www.ICGtesting.com
Printed in the USA
LVOW09s1608060217

523352LV00021B/945/P

9 781279 272657